Horoscope

Beginners Guide on Astrology and Signs

(A Four Step Approach to Interpret Horoscopes Using Vedic Methodology)

Melvin Pettit

Published By **Bengion Cosalas**

Melvin Pettit

All Rights Reserved

Horoscope: Beginners Guide on Astrology and Signs (A Four Step Approach to Interpret Horoscopes Using Vedic Methodology)

ISBN 978-1-7770663-8-3

No part of this guidebook shall be reproduced in any form without permission in writing from the publisher except in the case of brief quotations embodied in critical articles or reviews.

Legal & Disclaimer

The information contained in this book is not designed to replace or take the place of any form of medicine or professional medical advice. The information in this book has been provided for educational & entertainment purposes only.

The information contained in this book has been compiled from sources deemed reliable, and it is accurate to the best of the Author's knowledge; however, the Author cannot guarantee its accuracy and validity and cannot be held liable for any errors or omissions. Changes are periodically made to this book. You must consult your doctor or get professional medical advice before using any of the suggested remedies, techniques, or information in this book.

Upon using the information contained in this book, you agree to hold harmless the Author from and against any damages, costs, and expenses, including any legal fees potentially resulting from the application of any of the information provided by this guide. This disclaimer applies to any damages or injury caused by the use and application, whether directly or indirectly, of any advice or information presented, whether for breach of contract, tort, negligence, personal injury, criminal intent, or under any other cause of action.

You agree to accept all risks of using the information presented inside this book. You need to consult a professional medical practitioner in order to ensure you are both able and healthy enough to participate in this program.

Table Of Contents

Chapter 1: Astrological Analysis "Horoscope" 1

Chapter 2: Know Your Children Ascendants 11

Chapter 3: Work And Fitness 22

Chapter 4: Public Status, Career, Repute 42

Chapter 5: The Cancer—Ascendant Personality 64

Chapter 6: Communication With The Environment 83

Chapter 7: Possession And Personal Security... 99

Chapter 8: Astrology – Where Starts Everything From… 121

Chapter 9: Astrology—Why Believe In It? 131

Chapter 10: Horoscope – My Authentic Self.. 151

Chapter 11: Constructive Elements Of The Horoscope 158

Chapter 12: Astrology And Psychology – The Balance Between Spirit, Soul And Body 166

Chapter 13: Birth Of The Hero 173

Chapter 1: Astrological Analysis "Horoscope"

Ascendant personalities of infants and adults

It is not enough to describe "you" simply as

Aries is one of the twelve Sun Signs characters. You are an individual, a unique personality. Quite obviously you can't be lumped in with millions of others born all over the world in the same month and told: "That is you". Astrology is not that superficial, it is true and often uncannily accurate. Take note that no two people born under the same Sign are identical. Each type is subject to numerous modifications such as nationality, colour, environment and heredity.

The king's daughter and the underprivileged child born at the same moment in the palace and slum will have the same basic thinking and urges, but their vastly different circumstances, conditions and karma will modify the essential purity of the type.

"Free Will" And Astrology

Does Astrology preclude "Free Will"? This is a question that concerns many people when they begin to understand the cosmic significance. One of the problems is that many of us misunderstand choice for "Free Will". Astrology shows that there is more than a considerable difference between the two. We all know that at any moment of choice we are free. Otherwise, we will not perform as human beings. We may have a reason for feeling one thing and choosing to do another fear, consideration for someone, love-but we are free to choose when the opportunity is presented. Only this is a very limited freedom. A person's choice amounts to, will I or won't I stop or go? speak or be silent? say yes or no? Two alternatives This limited choosing certainly could not be required with freedom. This limited choosing where we feel the burden of our worldly obligations and frequently choose the way of duty rather than what we feel is right for us is presented by the Ascendants Sign. You will remember that this is the second most important factor in the Horoscope; the character and the personality we show to the world and our environment— rich or poor, orphaned or cherished healthy or unhealthy is determined by the Earths relation to the Zodiac at the moment of birth. The limited choice is limited freedom, the condition of our worldly existence. Horoscope is limited freedom and Free Will is unlimited freedom and abnormal. "Absolute freedom is inhuman". If a man or a woman is not handsome and beautiful (good character, good hygiene) at 20; not strong (able to stand up with food on the table, independent) at 30; not wise (capable to get home, get married) at 40; not wealthy (capable to own a property, take full responsibility for the family) at 50, he or she is "done".

KARMA "You must reap what you sow"

(good or bad; love or hate; heaven or hell). It is the good karma that takes a person to a life of bliss to wit. Good health; enjoyed wealth; fitness, happiness; long life with joy (heaven).

Bad karma takes a person to prison; ill-health of various diseases; protracted illness; poverty; untimely death (hell).

Reference St. John 5:2-14 Jesus at the pool of Bethesda.

2. Now there is at Jerusalem by the shipping market a pool, which is called in the Hebrew tongue Bethesda having five porches.

3. In these lay a great multitude of impotent folk of blind, halt, withered, waiting for the moving of the water.

4. For an angel went down at a certain season into the pool, and troubled the water; whosoever then after the troubling of the water stepped in was made whole of whatever disease he had

5. And a certain man was there, which had an infirmity thirty and eight (38) years

6. When Jesus saw him lie, and new that he had been now a long time in that case; He said unto him, will thou be made whole?

7. The impotent man answered him, Sir I have no man, when the water is troubled, to put me into the pool; but while I am coming, another steppeth down before me.

8. Jesus saith unto him, Rise to take up thy bed and walk.

14. Afterward Jesus findeth him in the temple, and said unto him, Behold, thou art made whole: sin no less a worse thing will come unto thee."

This statement by Jesus at the temple proves to the entire world that heaven and hell are experienced on this earth. Both soul and body enjoy heaven and so also suffer hell when sin is committed. It all means that at death the soul leaves the body to go to rest. The strange belief that there is heaven or hell after death should be discarded as phoney. If you know your basic character traits and potentialities (Sun Sign), your likely pattern of behaviour and the risks and benefits that may flow there from (the planets), combined with the advantage of seeing yourself as you appear to others (Ascendant), you will be in a much better position to assert your talents, correct your short-comings, exploit your natural possibilities, bring greater harmony into your relationships with others—in short, to live a richer and more meaningful life devoid of meddling by reverends, pastors, prophets and Imam. You then don't have to seek salvation in strange beliefs and doctrines from churches, prayer houses, mosques etc. With the knowledge, you will be "yourself". And to the degree that this self-realization becomes permanent and profound you will be the master of your fate, and stable personality and an individual well worth having around.

Compatibility Guide

ARIES - RAM - March 21—April 20

TAURUS - BULL - April 21—May 20

GEMINI - TWINS - May 21—June 20

CANCER - CRAB - June 21—July 20

LEO - LION - July 21—August 21

VIRGO - VIRGIN - August 22—Sept. 22

LIBRA - SCALES - Sept. 23—Oct. 22

SCORPIO - SCORPION - Oct. 23 - Nov. 22

SAGITTARIUS - ARCHER - Nov. 23 - Dec. 20

CAPRICORN - GOAT - Dec. 21—Jan. 19

AQUARIUS - WATER-BEARER - Jan. 20-Feb. 18

PISCES - FISHES - Feb. 18—Mar. 20

Natural Marriage Guide

This guide is for a happy and long-lasting marriage, choosing a partner compatible that makes "For better, for worse, till death do us part."

ARIES

Most Compatible Signs: Leo and Sagittarius.

Next Best: Taurus, Gemini, Pisces and Aquarius.

TAURUS

Most Compatible Signs: Virgo and Capricorn.

Next Best: Gemini, Cancer, Pieces and Aries.

GEMINI

Most Compatible Signs: Libra and Aquarius.

Next Best: Cancer, Leo, Aries and Taurus.

CANCER

Most Compatible Signs: Scorpion and Pisces.

Next Best: Leo, Virgo, Taurus and Gemini.

LEO

Most Compatible Signs: Sagittarius and Aries.

Next Best: Virgo, Libra, Gemini and Cancer.

VIRGO

Most Compatible Signs: Capricorn and Taurus.

Next Best: Libra, Scorpio, Leo and Cancer.

LIBRA

Most Compatible Signs: Aquarius and Gemini. Next Best: Scorpio, Sagittarius, Leo, and Virgo.

SCORPIO

Most Compatible Signs: Pieces and Cancer. Next Best: Sagittarius, Capricorn, Virgo and Libra.

SAGITTARIUS

Most Compatible Signs: Aries and Leo. Next

Best: Capricorn, Aquarius, Libra and Scorpion.

CAPRICORN

Most Compatible Signs: Taurus and Virgo. Next Best: Aquarius, Pisces, Scorpio and Sagittarius.

AQUARIUS

Most Compatible Signs: Gemini and Libra. Next Best: Sagittarius, Capricorn, Pisces and Aries.

PISCES

Most Compatible Signs: Cancer and Scorpio. Next Best: Capricorn, Aquarius, Aries and Taurus.

"Astrology is astronomy brought to earth and applied to the affairs of man." Emerson

Chapter 2: Know Your Children Ascendants

The following descriptions of children born under the various Signs are based on the position of the Sun, the most powerful influence in the horoscope. Most individuals conform to the solar influence. However, variations do occur because of the placement of the other planets at the time of birth. And of course, the birth Signs of the parents will also be reflected in the child's conditioning. "The apple does not fall far from its tree." Naturally, children inherit something good or bad from their parents.

For a closer examination of these factors, it is advisable to study the individual child's and the parents' horoscopes, which are available for every Sign in Astrological Analysis. All you need to know is the person's date of birth.

Since some Signs are naturally more or less compatible with others, you can obtain a further idea of how children and parents will hit it off by referring to the Compatibility

Guide and Ascendant personality.

THE ARIES CHILD MARCH 21 TO APRIL 20

The Aries child is extremely bright (sometimes brilliant) and usually very advanced for his or her age.

Too much applause and reference to the child's character by admiring adults is likely to make him strive to outdo himself and overstress his nervous system. This could result in sleeplessness, super sensitivity and an overcritical approach to his playmates and later all his associates. The Aries child is obstinate and needs to be intelligently quieted. His mind is so alert to the possibilities for action in his environment that he finds it difficult to concentrate on one thing for very long. He begins new interests with great enthusiasm but usually veers off well before they are finished. Sometimes it is because he has discovered the challenge is within his capabilities and so loses interest in it. But if a toy or game is beyond him, he will petulantly turn his back on it or perhaps break it or throw it away. He should be taught to apply himself to finish what he starts. The chances of success will be greater in an atmosphere where he feels there is due recognition of the importance of what he is doing.

From the start, these youngsters should be taught the advantages of slowing down without inhibiting their spontaneity. Their excited, sudden movements are apt to lead to more than their share of accidents. They will usually be recovering from a bruise, scald or cut somewhere on their body. Aries boys and girls need to be physically active; it helps to work off the excess nervous energy that subtracts from their powers of concentration. But they need to learn the value of deliberate, measured movement as against unrestrained hustle and bustle; their parents should inculcate in them a sense of the grace of rhythm, which their impulsive actions seldom allow.

Sports are good for the Aries child and he or she is usually proficient at them. It is wise to have children coached from an early age so that they express themselves with style and expertise. Abounding energy and desire to succeed will prevent them from becoming performing cogs in a wheel. Either they'll get to the top of the team or they'll quit and try another activity until they make their mark.

In none of his activities should the Arieschild be encouraged to show off? If restraint or discipline is required, it should be exercised tactfully so it won't injure the youngster's pride. Aries is a fiercely proud sign, and this is the key to the nobility that can readily be developed in this character.

It is important that this type of child be allowed to discover things for himself and not constantly be told what to do. He likes to experiment. Too much supervision and interference make him resentful. He learns from making mistakes. He might make the same mistake more than once (which can be rather exasperating for a parent), but this is his style. He packs a lot of experience into his life. He is attracted by the challenge rather than by the result.

The Aries child often reveals creative talents quite early These should be nurtured and developed as soon as they appear, without stressing the competitive angle.

One of the main problems is an overactive imagination. Young Aries should be taught not to exaggerate and to learn to describe objects and events as they are, not as he or she fancies them to be.

The aries ascendant personality

You who were born with Aries ascending are lovers of action. You want to be out in front. You are the pioneering impulse of mankind. As soon as you get a good idea, you immediately try to put it into action. Since you are so impulsive, you will spend some time licking your wounds because you failed to make a thorough evaluation of the opposition or obstacles. But you are not easily discouraged from the beginning again. You are at your best when you can lay down a plan of action for yourself and others to follow. Your mode of operation is to move on to greener pastures before the task is finished, leaving others to press on or clean up. You enjoy a position of command. You can guide, control and govern yourself as well as others. You are an admirer of scientific thought and have some distinct philosophical leanings. You are a lover of independence who does not like sharing your secrets or revealing your plans. You prefer to demonstrate your tactical inspiration in activity rather than talk about what you intend to do.

Like a good general (Mars is the ruler of Aries ascending), you don't like to risk having your plans fall into enemy hands. You possess strong and penetrating willpower. You are quite versatile, able to change from one activity to another without losing a bit as long as your interest is sustained. You sometimes miss out on the rewards of your considerable efforts because you moved before they were handed out. You are enterprising and ambitious and usually headstrong. You reach out eagerly for what you want, but you are easily put off by complicated situations that might slow your progress. You react indignantly if imposed upon or abused and are apt to speak out and let others know quickly that they have offended you. Your temper can be quite fiery, but you don't hold grudges for long. You prefer to settle differences quickly and get your battles over in a hurry, which way the result may go. You are brimful of initiative and make an able executive, though you may lack persistence.

Quite often you are interested in physical sports and your physique reflects this. You will do best in a vocation that requires instant decisions and action.

Possessions and personal protection

You are probable to be high-quality at acquiring assets, mainly land and homes. You don't permit cash to lie idle in the financial agency; you will as an alternative make investments it within the bricks and mortar. Tangible assets that provide you with a strong hold inside the worldwide are what you need most.

In industrial organisation, wherein you also are prone to be impulsive you are probably to strength a tough bargain. You are extra conservative in economic topics than in most others. You spend cash to boom the charge of your house. You don't permit some issue you private to fall into disrepair, and that includes your frame. You are health-conscious and genuinely aware about the want to preserve your body in form.

Communication with the surroundings

You are apt to scramble your terms at instances due to the fact your tongue can't keep up with the charge of your idea. Your expressive Aries speech may additionally moreover amplify a stammer whilst you are excited or immoderate. You may be accused of opportunism because you can certainly see the validity of several humans's factors of view right now. You have a tendency to be hasty or explosive in speech at the same time as protective your self. The unguarded phrase can also give you motive for remorse. You are careworn and impatient, eager for emblem spanking new conferences. Your innovative thoughts impress the ones you discern for. You are at the pass masses and can be inclined to stumble or knock matters over.

Home, Family, And Tradition

You are very sentimental approximately your family. Your mom or any other near elder has a totally precise place in your coronary coronary heart. Your home technique a exceptional deal to you. If you have not settled down you prolonged to do so and often recollect it. You count on plenty about the beyond. You are an admirer of manner of lifestyles and the coolest vintage days. You are fund of studying approximately facts and archaeological topics; you could moreover show this interest physically via travelling museums and even taking component in digs at antique ruins. You can also make severa changes of residence before locating the residence you're looking for. You paintings hard at making your home a cushty area to head away in.

Self-expression, love life, leisure

You have a longing to be observed applauded. Your Aries aggressiveness also can reason others to accuse you of being bossy or dictatorial. You take satisfaction in dramatizing your efforts in generating mind-blowing outcomes. Your accomplishments are thoughts-blowing. Your head can be grew to become through flattery and glamour.

An impatience to fulfil your ambition may additionally pressure you into taking risks, even though you usually hedge your bets to maintain your protection. You enjoy a wonderful time. Your amorous affairs are largely ego trips. You need to be proud of your kids and experience situations wherein you can display them (at the least the successful ones) off.

Chapter 3: Work And Fitness

You are a steady worker, despite the fact that no person will describe you as a plodder. You toil with deft power of mind. You can separate the chaff from the wheat with high-quality ease whether or not you're coping with human beings or element. You are green and disciplined in your personal existence. You are keenly aware of hygiene and now and again may be finicky. You experience delicacies but seldom devour or drink to more. You take more than not unusual care of your frame due to the fact accurate health technique you can stay active. Sickness irritates you, makes you worrying, and snappish. At instances you're too quick to find out fault with co-employees; however but traumatic, your criticisms are very regularly right to the mark.

Partnership and marriage

In this department, Aries is not an impartial loner. You need to percentage your existence with others, particularly a love accomplice.

You anticipate the admiration of your mate, and at times adoring interest. You attempt to get along facet your companions, Harmony is extremely vital to you, but you don't generally locate it. Your directness and now and again rugged manner may additionally additionally furthermore offend even your very own finer sensibilities. You enjoy the pull of internal extremes and are continuously striving to relaxation to your inner stability. You typically marry early after romantic formative years. Marriage to a properly matched and fascinating character is vital to you. You can be adamant, however at coronary coronary coronary heart, you are a peacemaker. Choose your rightful accomplice from "Compatibility Guide" on web web page

10 above Shared resources, legacies, intercourse

Secretive approximately your deeper feelings, you seldom interact in intimate discussions with outsiders. In your love existence, you're sensual rather than sentimental. You have severa secretes. You enjoy a want to upward push above the temptation of your lower nature, however the fact that this can be neither smooth nor for my part suitable. You are a powerhouse of emotional electricity that wants to be nicely harnessed. Sometimes a strenuous physical hobby will work off your extra strength. By sublimating your deeper drives, you can attain towering heights of attainment. You are a realist. You apprehend human failings. You don't like pretence. You can be torn through jealousy.

Higher improvement and long-distance journey

You have an interesting religious or philosophic outlook, regardless of the reality that not unconventional. You are looking for new vistas of the mind. You are specially clever and sometimes astound your friends together with your penetrative powers of notion. You are an expansive character, forever looking to widen your horizons. You want to tour afar to take in new cultures, meet one in all a kind kinds of people and come upon easy situations. You regularly do matters at the spur of the on the spot through percentage inspiration. Your fantastic, frank, and generous nature helps you to entice partners who have some thing out of the everyday to offer.

Public standing, profession, popularity

Your Aries expertise as an organizer on this characteristic fits you for big company. You are incredible of developing in your area, mainly in later lifestyles. You are accountable and ambitious, even though your techniques may be conservative.

You want to be identified as an professional because you don't need to take orders. You are capable of exquisite and enduring effort; patience proper right here is your long in form. You want to assume for others. You appear instead aloof and unfriendly, however that is surely your not unusual manner whilst vital topics should be attended to. You are happier in charge of the massive scene than coping with information, which you prefer to leave to others.

Friends, agencies sports activities, want, desires

Your Aries love of independence can be overemphasized right proper right here. You can also kick up your heels, damage a few traditions, and determined on friends who do the identical. But your industrial organization partners might be greater conventional, you've got were given the knack of coping properly with the two extremes. You are a piece modern, greater highbrow than sentimental. Your advanced thoughts may additionally appeal to three weird- bodes. You need to express your broader views freely, and the bohemian varieties of this worldwide are the most receptive listeners. You are tolerant of various's eccentricities. Your aptitude for originality is tremendous; you shine in business enterprise sports.

Hidden reasons, selfless company, psychic

emotions

You are instinctively capable of decide the proper issue to do. Although you will be impulsive, your actions will possibly turn out for the fine. You have a completely easy component for your nature, which you can unconsciously repress. Any excessively sympathetic responses you manipulate to manipulate in a unmarried way will erupt into compulsive movement in some other. You may also moreover have problem know-how some of your emotional reactions. The plight of the struggling of fellow guy is apt to move you to actions of self-denial. You also can additionally enjoy a want and introspection, but seldom be capable of find out the time for each. Your instinct is acute.

THE TAURUS CHILD - APRIL 21 TO

MAY 20

Taurus is usually a adorable infant, each to examine and in disposition. But he has some very specific characteristics that aren't immediately discernible. These need to be understood, mainly through his instructors, for him to expand in a everyday, balanced way.

Above everything else, more youthful Taureans need love and affection. They are deeply sensitive and unsure of themselves inner. They often deliver the advent of being splendidly self-assured, however this is to seize up on their uncertainty, which could quantity nearly to an inferiority complex at times.

Taureans are not highbrow beings, basically. They stay on their feelings, which need to be continuously stimulated via the demonstration and knowledge that they are cherished and favored. You can't just inform a Taurus little one which you love him or her. You have to reveal it in physical phrases via cuddling and petting or with being involved moves. If you don't try this, the kid turns into increasingly more indifferent, and as he receives older, will flip to sensual self-indulgence as an alternative for the loving stimulation he left out as a infant. Failing this, Taurus may also moreover additionally grow to be increasingly more stolid, and, in maturity, a as an alternative silly and dull individual.

Young Taurus has incredible willpower, which might also moreover moreover, at times, show itself as a nervous obstinacy. If he digs in his toes, no argument or hazard will shake him. He can be unreasonable. Again, most effective an attraction to his emotional self is apt to make him relent. Should he ever lose his mood, it could be a devastatingly memorable event.

He is a certainly modest toddler and has a tendency to underrate his skills. He should not be criticized to make him "do higher" because of the truth complaint will handiest make him experience greater inferior and then, probably, defiantly overconfident and at risk of making silly errors. He responds an entire lot better to reward and encouragement.

Taurus kids are not studious kinds. Normal schooling strategies don't paintings so properly with them. To check, they ought to have their emotions aroused in order to take a actual hobby inside the assignment. These boys and women want to narrate to subjects through their senses; inside the event that they're to discover about nature, they ought to test the specimen, contact it, odor it. With arithmetic and considered one of a kind precis subjects, the teacher should discover a manner of exciting them into participation with demonstrations, models. The failure to understand this regularly outcomes in branding the Taurus toddler as a sluggish learner, whilst he's in truth, not anything of the kind.

Friendship and playmates are very important to Taurean children If they may be capable of't combination with kids they select, they will slow down bodily and mentally, and may with out problem become lazy and detached. Having a super love of delight (as it lets in them learn how to be highbrow creatures), they may pick out partners who teach them awful conduct.

Properly dealt with and endorsed, the Taurus infant fast locations aside his timidity and will become a nice and congenial little character. He is probably to be innovative together along with his hands and any signal of this must be cultivated.

The Taurus - ascendant character

You who were born with Taurus ascending are self-reliant people able to going for walks tough for prolonged intervals to accomplish the desires you region for yourself. You also are remarkable at running for others. You are an ideal man or woman to have at the payroll, you have got a flair for earning money for whoever employs you.

You generally own a pleasant or attractively super voice. You supply an have an effect on of grace and compact motion, no matter the fact that a number of you may be at the obese facet. You like gold—simply. You attempt to acquire cash so you can convert it into stable assets. Nothing ought to please you extra than to very personal a gold mine, for the sheer, deliciously strong feeling of it. You don't like taking risks with what you private. You might as an opportunity rely on your sensible capacity for dogged try than take a huge win-or-lose chance.

You are a moderate person at coronary coronary heart and don't go searching out hassle. You aren't easy to initiate to anger however as fast as stirred, your rage can be bold. When you are negative you could show great stubbornness.

It is this unyielding outstanding that allows you to grasp on like a bulldog to obligations and reasons that could daunt each extraordinary type inside the Zodiac. Once you're making up your thoughts, this is the prevent of it, you keep on with your desire through thick and skinny. There is a great deal of latent power within the returned of your powers of staying electricity. But if it's far out of location, you may be overly sensual, too depending on consolation, and indolent. You are honest, reliable, and easy. You have a bargain of commonplace revel in. You make a totally reliable friend. You have a flair for financial manipulation and enormous organizing potential, as a manner to be useful for your profession, You need time to count on topics over, weigh all of the experts and cons in advance than conducting a selection, and due to this, others every now and then regard you as ponderous and sluggish. You have a compelling want to get the whole thing on a firm basis earlier than intending. You are as an alternative secretive and reserved regarding your non-public affairs.

Although typically of a quiet disposition, you can be specially dogmatic. You are deeply stimulated through sympathy. You love beauty in nature, song, literature, or artwork. You also are fund of pleasure and the comforts of this international. You are keen to surround yourself with lovable subjects. Good food and refinements of interesting that go along with it are important to you. You are a most snug man or woman and can have a calming and useful effect on parents which are worried or irritable. Although affectionate and loving, you will be exasperatingly unreasonable and prejudiced.

Possessions and private safety

You set your mind to earning income. You don't forget specific schemes, trying out them along side your big powers of imagination to make certain they art work earlier than setting them into movement. You are very likely to on more method to beautify your income. You use wit and intelligence to diversify your financial pastimes in order that your protection is never without a doubt vulnerable. Money generally involves you thru severa channels. You like to domesticate the friendship of human beings with wealth and cloth possessions. Since you furthermore mght like to offer the effect that you are doing well yourself, you don't thoughts spending cash on presents, traveling, and different communications.

Communication with the environment

You are in normal touch collectively along with your closest own family. You have an urgent need to understand that every one is well with people who love you and with the ones to whom you experience associated. You are sensitive on your surroundings mainly to the neighbourhood in which you stay. If your house is not in a suitable area, you are unhappy. Although you're unsettled thru a idea of a major alternate, you may in all likelihood skip residence extra than as quickly as to find the proper environment. Un interfering with neighbours may be a big attention. Just as Taurus youngsters have a observe a whole lot faster if the mission is given emotional this means that, you absorb knowledge slowly however sincerely, as soon as the sensation is right.

Home, own family, subculture

Your domestic is your castle and you depart no doubt in all of us's thoughts which you need to be the lord or woman of it. Domestic existence possibly revolves round your options, however the truth that there can be others to bear in mind. You like to dispense hospitality from a properly-stocked larder and an first rate wine cellar (or rack). You are an interesting and gracious host with a flair for supplying lavish and glamorous prospers. If you could manipulate, you may buy your self a mansion, fill it with high priced topics and arrange an endless parade of admiring traffic. If "home" is the fine cave, you'll be depended upon to make it snug, outstanding, and homelike.

Self-expression, love life, entertainment You experience love affairs but they don't obsess your questioning. You are not keen on romantic having a pipe dream or colouring your relationships with imagination. You consider in having the whole thing in its proper region, and that consists of your emotions. You can be a bit prudish and critical of modern permissiveness. You pick out a love mate with first-rate warning, however once having made your self-control, you want to get on with what takes area subsequent so that you'll constantly realize what is going on subsequent. You are a piece too methodical for spontaneous gamesmanship. A stimulating discussion or an hobby highlighting meals is frequently your concept of amusement. Strenuous video video games or sports activities activities don't enchantment to you.

Work and fitness

You need to paintings in harmonious conditions. Any diploma of discord will throw you off stability and ship you taking walks for exit or the escapist's bottle. Your fitness depends very an awful lot on your being able to preserve an amicable and agreeable atmosphere spherical you. You paintings thoroughly with others. You are cooperative, suitable-natured, and happy. Tact and international individuals of the family are your unique trends. You are organized to work as one of the organization and may frequently manage to deliver together warring factions. Peace at almost any fee is your slogan. But on occasion your exactitude irritates co-employees. Your art work is regularly in fields that require a innovative touch.

Partnership and marriage

You are in all likelihood a pretty demanding marriage associate because of the truth you pour the full-size intensity of your feelings into your closest relationships. Jealousy and possessiveness can make life miserable at instances for you every. You are lots happier in case you experience a nice sexual dating along facet your married companion. Disloyalty through using the alternative person might also have deep intellectual repercussions. Partnership for you is a intense employer and also you don't shirk from sharing your fabric wealth and method with those you live with. Your intuition acts like a sixth feel wherein partners are involved. Although you're strongly physical, you need someone with intellectual talents as well. Choose your rightful accomplice from "Most Compatible Signs", above.

Shared property, legacies, intercourse

You are apt to gain from inheritance of cash, property, or name. The completing of a partnership may be in particular worthwhile in cloth phrases. Big industrial agency settlements can also moreover moreover all of sudden have an impact on and coincide with an abrupt exchange in your manner of lifestyles. You have a sturdy social sense of proper and wrong approximately the manner human beings address the inexperienced instinct and the effect of this on the community. You take delivery of as actual with in the ethical law, and that is pondered for your lofty ethics concerning intercourse. Whatever freedoms you may seem to take in sexual hobby, you can check strict thoughts of your very personal. You believe in a life hereafter.

Higher improvement and prolonged-distance excursion

Although your religious beliefs will be predisposed to be traditional, you have the depth to spite others to enlightenment probably greater than your non-public. You are conservative and alternatively orthodox for your opinions about the deeper questions of existence. You are organized to simply accept or stay with doctrines handed down from the beyond until a few authority proves they'll be wrong or lays down an possibility.

You don't enjoy speculating approximately philosophic possibilities and you're a chunk suspicious of individuals who do. Like the lawyer (a profession in which you must shine), you want concrete evidence in advance than committing yourself. Travel doesn't commonly keep precise attraction till it's far connected with exchange.

Chapter 4: Public Status, Career, Repute

You experience greater regular and happy in a profession in that you parent with a set. You have thousands to contribute being, every a cohesive and chronic have an impact on further to an particular logician. You need to sense you are doing an tremendous system and are pulling your weight. Emotionally, you're more worried with the purpose than with the people worried. Your ideas are frequently modern. You may be an succesful inventor. Science can also provide a place where you could artwork with delight and renown within the route of fixing mankind's graver problems. You are organized to sacrifice hundreds for the greater purpose. You are a tireless employee for the species in preference to for an man or woman.

Friends, institution sports, hopes, desires You have real buddies, the sorts who don't neglect about you regardless of the reality that you could seldom meet. You really need to understand all of your friends, but you are particular approximately who gets near you.

You get alongside well with people. You are organized to concentrate to their issues with out in search of to introduce your non-public. You have a deep reservoir of sympathy in your fellow man or woman, in particular for the underdog, the underprivileged, and the sick. You rely upon your partners a excellent deal to fill your need for emotional sharing. You are more results hurt than maximum if you sense your pals are neglecting you. You recognize with struggling people and aren't beyond a grand but unostentatious gesture of self-denial on their behalf.

Hidden motives, selfless company, psychic

feelings

You provoke as many moves as you may backstage. You don't announce what you are as masses as until you need to. The façade you present to the general public every now and then bears little resemblance to the person internal. A sympathetic, active, and frequently mystery creativeness plots the course to your compelling actions. You revel in on occasion that your picks are made for you. This is the dynamic aspect inside the Zodiac from wherein all of your Taurean interest stems. The function offers the strength to repress impatience and to be as an opportunity lengthy-struggling. Once your anger flares, it could end up a self-paralyzing fury that explodes internal you, causing debilitating consequences greater risky than suppressing your anger.

THE GEMINI CHILD MAY 21 TO JUNE 20

Gemini kids are typically full of confused, worried power. It comes from their minds, which can be like delicately tuned digital devices. They in truth can't maintain regardless of the truth that mentally or bodily. They need to be constantly engaged in some thing that hobbies them. Parents and instructors may additionally additionally moreover find this an onerous enterprise, mainly because those lovely little imps get bored more speedy than maximum children.

And on the same time as that occurs, and no man or woman's spherical, their ability for mischief is nearly amazing.

Young Gemini is a totally super little one. He or she learns without delay and has an alert, inquiring thoughts that needs to recognize the purpose inside the once more of the whole thing that catches his or her attention.

As regularly as realistic, Gemini youngsters need to be spoke back factually and now not eliminate because of the truth the question takes place to be inappropriate. This is the way they soak up, and every fact goes into their formidable memory, in which it is going to be recalled as quickly because it's required. In a totally brief time, you may train a Gemini little one nearly a few element.

He might not be bodily robust in his early years because of the truth his complete device is beneath the continual anxiety of fever worried hobby. As his body adapts to this, he's going to get stronger, till in the end, in maturity, his health might be dictated in big part by way of his kingdom of thoughts.

Just as Gemini can degree terrific recoveries at the same time as new and novel pastimes appear, so he can become listless whilst assailed with the beneficial aid of boredom and depression.

The natural Gemini infant needs plenty of physical activities, but usually not in the form of hard and strenuous sports sports activities. His narrow, agile body and short actions permit him to excel in games requiring idea and method in area of brute strength and persistence.

It is especially critical for the ones boys and women to get as heaps sleep and rest as viable. But that is typically less complicated said than organized. At bedtime, the cause should be to keep away from satisfaction that stimulates the imagination. Stories and tv suggests must be cautiously decided on. Horror movies etc are nearly certain to cause nightmares and excessive anxiety. The toddler can be scared of the darkish properly into his or her teenagers.

Gemini kids often exaggerate and inform outrageous lies with great plausibility. Their creativeness is so energetic and vibrant that they live out adventures and dramas of their heads and can't (or would in all likelihood alternatively now not) separate fiction from fact.

They make wonderful actors, capable of mimic sounds and reproduce the traits of people they examine. Sometimes the ones children be afflicted through way of a mild speech impediment the mind is in reality too speedy for the vocal device. But with staying strength and information, this can be triumph over. Otherwise, the Gemini toddler is generally properly advanced in his speech and comprehension. He can be a horrible chatterbox, notwithstanding the reality that.

A toddler of this Sign is more intellectual than sentimental and may once in a while be gradual at displaying love and affection.

The Gemini—Ascendant Personality

With Gemini ascending, you should be continuously busy to be satisfied. You crave alternate and variety; deprive you of these, and life loses its that means. You have a mental life. Your global is the arena of mind. You unrealistically anticipate your bodily environment to transport at the identical pace as your thoughts; consequently you're frequently bored and careworn.

You are bold and curious. You intention to broaden an inquiring mind and brief wit: the ones are the implements you operate to get earlier and to protect your self the instantaneous problem looms. You are not a very bodily entity. You use your frame as u use your thoughts, every so often riding it to a state of close to exhaustion."Jack be nimble, Jack is brief, Jack leap over the candle stick"— is you! A generally slim and agile frame permits you to move with pace and flowing precision.

You are sympathetic and sensitive, very quick to pick out the mind and attitudes of others. Your lucid perception is often improper for intuition, but you are basically an intellectual creature. Being really an idealist, you frequently experience you may remedy the troubles of the arena on your head. You are not past assisting a extremely good purpose nearly, particularly if you could take at the interest of transport up enthusiasm and useful useful resource with letters, telephones calls, and the private electricity of your rhetoric.

You like pride and journey. Your fertile creativeness is always at paintings, trying to introduce novelty into your sports. You revel in all forms of highbrow endeavor, which consist of mind-teaser video video games. You are interested in experimentation and studies. Education in its wider experience draws you and you'll soak up a have a look at to amuse your self or actually stay knowledgeable. You are attracted through manner of medical subjects because of the fact they're involved with facts and people are greater important to you, essentially than critiques. You are pretty adaptable and may tailor your verbal exchange and language to suit any corporation business enterprise you seem like in. You like to talk. To others, you seem to have an remarkable zest for living and your buddies are regularly amazed at the way you preserve your more youthful outlook. Like Peter Pan, you don't appear to expand antique as normal mortals do. As lengthy as you're fired with the aid of manner of enthusiasm's vital spark, you appear in case you want to transport on all of the time, dancing from challenge to project, never appearing to weary of incessant range. At instances you turn out to be hectic, careworn, and indecisive. You also can be mentally timid. When inactive, you come to be impatient and irritable. Your immoderate-robust nature makes you distinctly excitable. You own the inherent literary capacity and are keen on reading and writing. You are quick to investigate and each respect or enjoy tune, painting, drawing, languages, adventure, and most forms of innovation and invention. You are able to doing severa subjects proper now and are awesome at wearing on an clever verbal exchange and deftly the usage of your fingers on the equal time.

Possessions and private protection

You are wonderful at growing your earnings and building up property in conditions in which you can enchantment to people's feelings specifically in their homes. You can be a hit in this manner thru tv, magazines, newspapers, books, and radio. You also can be a con artist.

You have a eager enjoy of values. You can prosper in change and alternate, specially inside the characteristic of agent or intermediary. You try to preserve your property and don't throw your coins spherical besides on occasion while you're chasing delight. You want to make your home comfortable and to provide properly on your circle of relatives. In doing this you, every so often appear like extravagant.

Communication with the surroundings

You have a outstanding talent for expressing yourself, for commanding the attention of others with a dash of showmanship. You aren't excellent a fluent talker and author you have got got were given style and presence that come thru, but, you pick out to talk. Writing and speaking, to you, arts that exist not nice for persuading others and moreover for gaining their admiration and recognize. You are the journalist who no longer first-class receives the interior song but who additionally feel that conveys the surroundings; the fun storyteller, the exciting public speaker, the absorbing lecturer. Sometimes you get over excited and on your enthusiasm, exaggerate present fiction as fact, and moreover say the wrong trouble.

Home, own family, way of life

You are a tidy individual and your own home shows this. You like orderliness and cleanliness. You will prefer to earn your residing with the resource of strolling at home, and this idea is frequently on your head as you methodically strive to higher yourself. You revel in it is important to fitness to go away in non violent environment wherein you may get higher quick from the rigours of your regular communique with the outside worldwide. The america will regularly fit you so long as you have got smooth get admission to to the brighter lighting fixtures.

You are a much deeper person than your flippant communication on occasion suggests. You can be pretty sharp on your appropriate, with family contributors who step out of line.

Self-expression, love life, enjoyment You like a super stability for your sports activities and manage to combine sociability, creativity, and going for walks with large dexterity. It isn't always beyond you to visit art work, supply a celebration and bring a few thing of innovative gain at the same day. You intend to act in socially appropriate techniques however it isn't unknown as a manner to every now and then burst off the wall whilst your spontaneity and exuberance get the better of you. You enjoy the agency of innovative people and own a flare for dressing well or stylishly every in conventional or contemporary mode. You are well-known with youngsters and have a gift for talking with them in vicinity of at them. In your love existence, you are a roamer and might have or 3 affairs going right now.

Work and fitness

You have a super expertise for ferreting out information and you do nicely in any profession or situation that wishes this functionality. You are nicely suitable for laboratory artwork, medical research packages, psychiatry, psychology, and investigative journalism. You can reduce through minutiae with razor-sharp keenness and reveal the reality that lies within the once more of it. In your art work, you may conquer your natural Gemini flippancy and grow to be deeply worried. A dedicated strive is not past you. You are regularly revitalized with the aid of the usage of unremitting endeavours. Co-folks who provoke you can enjoy the brink of your tongue.

Partnership and marriage

You marry more for intellectual than physical reasons. You are happiest with a associate who's intellectually remarkable and able to proportion your ideas. Sex is secondary in your want to be understood by way of way of your associate, to experience that your highbrow limitations are being constantly driven yet again thru the near contact among two smart humans. You gained't be nagged and you received't be imprisoned, you may instead be single. You want a mate who can handle your affairs and offer the enjoy of motive which you require, with out proscribing your freedom and scope for self-expression. It is a tall order. In flip, you provide a totally adaptable witty, communicative and hopeful personality. Choose your rightful companion from the "Compatibility Guide" on net web page 10 above.

Shared property, legacies, intercourse

Your sex lifestyles is plain reduce and you may preserve it proportional for your special pursuits. You seldom, have some distinct severe draw close-u.S.A. Of americaapproximately intercourse; you aren't a sentimental type and your method is surely rely-of-fact. You generally should wait till rather past due in existence to gain from legacies. Sentiments are regularly not on time. Your views on an afterlife are conservative and you haven't any excellent choice to invest approximately demise. Your interest in occult subjects, however, may be quite excessive and you've got got an inherent ability for digging out the truth. You revel in exposing trickery.

Higher improvement and prolonged-distance

adventure

You are seldom a conformist in your spiritual ideals. You think that the truths contained in the traditional religions may be expressed in rational phrases and require no mumbo-jumbo.

You enjoy that the set up church buildings need to hold up with the times. You have a incredible urge to percent your thoughts with as many people as feasible and to excursion long distances. You want to disseminate information. You cause to apprehend one of a kind races, to visit and live amongst them in case you get the danger, to study special cultures firsthand. You are tolerant of numerous humans's ideals and don't set out to transform them out of your very very own.

Public fame career, status

Your essential hassle in life is attempting to make up your thoughts approximately what you need to do with it. The trouble is that you could benefit fulfillment in pretty a whole lot any career that appeals to you which ones ones of them gives you little incentive to stick to one career. You in no way appear to discover the profession that would fulfill you for prolonged. Once you could deal with a job, have a propensity to transport on. Often you operate your versatility to follow multiple vocation simultaneously. You also can switch from one venture to every one of a kind, looking for the golden one that allows you to fulfil you. Some of you may as an alternative be drifters that settle for a monotonous or mundane function. Your search for a dream also can serve to reduce your immediately opportunities of reputation and renown.

Friends, companies sports, hopes, goals Friendship is one of the maximum essential spheres of your life. You have many pals and keep in everyday touch. Friendship approach variety, alternate communication, animation, movement, discussion-all of the matters you need most. As this department is the zodiacal point that offers upward thrust to Gemini interest thru organisation, you are notably proper at making buddies. You get to apprehend the proper people, have an aptitude for enlisting cooperation and are especially a achievement at beginning organization activities. You be part of subjects to satisfy others, and as speedy as that is achieved, often withdraw. You are apt to squander your energies marshalling help for too many projects proper away and run out of steam earlier than any is finished.

Hidden reasons, selfless provider, psychic

emotions

Although you could not display it, you're frequently shaken by using manner of a experience of fabric loss of confidence. You can also try and have an impact on a wonderful detachment from the topics of the arena, but below you fear about your economic institution account and try to positioned pennies apart for a rainy day. You are frequently a silent saver-busily, amongst other sports, stamping the earth spherical your cash chest. It is this vague anxiety approximately economic topics that account for plenty of your Mercurial versatility. You purpose unconsciously that the extra skills you may enlarge and feature at your disposal, the much less hazard there can be of falling on difficult times.

Your technique is once in a while devious.

THE CANCER CHILD JUNE 21 TO JULY 20

The Cancer little one appears for romance and a placid life. These boys and women are fairly touchy and timid. Even despite the fact that they crave to make friends, their retiring nature renders it difficult to make the primary drift. They do not revel in being on my own, they want to sense they belong. A Cancer infant will dangle tenaciously to every body who loves him. The maximum tough parental challenge is to push this touchy little creature lightly in advance into the world.

Although the Cancer infant is not the neatest or brightest of youngsters, he possesses innate capabilities that a practical upbringing will help make take area. The tendency for overdue development makes the teens quite important for them.

Young Cancer responds remarkably to adults who show they receive as genuine with in him. For folks who love him, he's going to do nearly some component. A responsive and understanding determine or instructor will try to arouse his hobby in video video games and sports activities that he can with a bit of achievement percent with one-of-a-kind kids. He want to now not be left to experience lonely. The object is to coax the child out, to make him greater impartial and outspoken. It is quality to encourage him to do as a superb deal as feasible for himself and allow him enjoy he's engaging in effects. These need to be praised and desired.

Cancer youngsters are wonderfully conscientious once they had been entrusted with a mission. Psychologically, the purpose for this is they're in normal need of approbation and examine speedy that one way of ensuring this is to do a manner assiduously.

These youngsters aren't studious and highbrow, despite the fact that they will come to be so in maturity. They have a look at thru their emotions. Unless they'll be very in reality associated with sensation, thoughts and thoughts confuse them. They need to smell a flower, sing a track, to taste a piece of fruit if they are going to gain information of about those items. You can't count on that a Cancer baby has were given the concept of a subject from a verbal description which could suffice for most special youngsters. Cancer is the Sign of the senses and intuition, so the child's intellectual development is predicated upon on emotional knowledge. Once a determine or teacher manages to arouse an soaking up hobby in him, the Cancer toddler also can moreover study himself to this difficulty for the rest of his lifestyles. Great resourceful and modern careers can be all began with the right remedy of those finely balanced little human beings Otherwise, the more youthful individual of this Sign is tempted to grow to be introverted and stay off his feelings moody, changeable and lethargic. Being in particular sensitive, the Cancer infant is effortlessly discouraged and takes complaint lots to coronary coronary heart. Worry can also disappointed his belly. He is also apt to be bothered by way of colds and chills. His fitness in his in advance years can be detached. He may also pick out at his meals and cry greater than most kids. Cancer kids are generally capable at making handicrafts. In later years, they regularly show an awesome aptitude for company coupled with an intensely formidable spirit.

Chapter 5: The Cancer—Ascendant Personality

If the Sign of Cancer turn out to be ascending on the hour of start, you are a person of converting moods and feelings. You are exceedingly sensitive and of retiring disposition. You recognize what it's far want to be damage and also you do your high-quality to shield those you like, especially your family from painful critiques. You are specially solicitous of your mother or matriarchal figures for your own family. Although situations may additionally additionally pressure you to lose contact with those humans. You are by no means absolutely freed from project for them. You have sturdy recollections of your teenagers. Whether your reminiscences are satisfied or unhappy, you could't help reminiscing. You are sentimental, sympathetic, and as an alternative talkative. Your creativeness is fertile and innovative. You experience first and assume after, even though to you it is almost useless. Your mind grow to be super "feeling" snap shots, with which you could end up privy to with extremely good pain or pleasure. Although you are eager on your house, you're willing to wander and may by no means truely manage to relax in a unmarried place. If you do no longer installation a everlasting house, you're apt to % and circulate off and bypass over again after two or 3 years. You have a amazing retentive memory, particularly for own family and historic occasions. You report away feeling in choice to concepts. As you have got a strong emotional attachment to the beyond, this possibly bills on your often incredible electricity of recall. You are keen on possessions and could paintings industriously to accumulate them. Your personal desires aren't wonderful and you will be very budget pleasant, even frugal, with cash. You want to adventure and revel in touring human beings of their houses. You are specifically susceptible to drop in on family. Novelty and alternate enchantment to you in almost any shape. Although you're cautious with cash, you are regularly imposed upon. Your sympathetic nature makes it tough at the way to refuse each other man or woman who appeals for assist or appears to be in want. But you've got a totally tenacious streak, which manifests itself in masses of techniques however it's far specially vehement at the identical time as you adopt a shielding position. You shrink back from stress. Can supply the effect of hardy self-assurance, and durability and might deal with the awesome of them for a confined length. But then you definately certainly must scuttle off to some heat and normal retreat wherein you may quietly restore your self warranty. You worry grievance and ridicule and could go to extraordinary lengths to avoid each. This makes you as a substitute conventional and discreet. You are willing to take a look at an career an amazing way to bring you in contact with the general public. You enjoy reward and approbation, this all yet again, makes you exceeding diplomatic. You are a lover of beauty and commonly own a psychic and mediumistic faculty.

Possessions And Personal Security

You like to do nicely so you can offer in your youngsters with fashion. You are one of the real collections of the Zodiac. You want to deliver collectively objects of paintings, gadgets of beautiful matters and relics of antiquity. You enjoy displacing these in your house for others to look. Your series is frequently valuable, however this is not a prerequisite, you are truly as able to saving worthless devices with the same affection and satisfaction due to the truth they provide you with a reassuring feeling of material protection. You are painfully affected while some thing you personal is broken or destroyed.

But no emotional scar hurts you for too prolonged.

Communication With The Environment

You are instead disturbing about the future so that you normally have a tendency to take shelter inside the beyond. You expect and talk masses about the coolest vintage days. You experience that traditional attitudes are more appropriate than current ones. You like to quote presidents. You take pride in your patriotism. You are often important of the thoughts of others and try and placed them on the proper music. You need to feel that you and your buddies are eating fitness-giving food. You collect dietary books and articles to help all concerned. Your eye for descriptive element is super. You often exaggerate your issues to yourself and worry unnecessarily.

Home, Family, Tradition

You regard your own home as the pivot of your life. As sentimental as you're approximately your own family, you may instead have an empty house than disturb it with discord and war of phrases. You purpose to keep concord to your environment and to accumulate this show tact and global members of the family to human beings with whom you live. If you fail to secure the balance you crave, you may depart the residence speedy or retire to the seclusion of your room. You spend lots of your entertainment time making your own home a greater attractive and congenial place to stay. You need to feel that your own family thinks and speaks properly of you on your absence.

Self-Expression, Love Life, Entertainment You are capable of producing artwork of superior inventive advantage, however to do this, you've got got to overcome a curious self-repressive tendency, this is to be brazenly possessive of your family, mainly your kids. You are willing to play a watchdog function, continually "guarding" or brooding over them, and this introverted centring of your emotional forces reduces your revolutionary fireside and proposal. In romance you veer in the course of mystery amorous affairs, finding exhilaration in the notion of tasting forbidden fruit and calculatedly ignoring the painful consequences that is probably worried. You can suffer deeply through jealousy, this is often matched thru using an depth of physical passion.

Work And Health

Your art work as an employee is marked thru an effective outlook that allows you to control cheerfully with large detail. As lengthy as you remember that what you're doing is beneficial and a step to larger things in the destiny, you'll workout your self with diligence. You are an industrious worker. In organizing and making plans, you use lesions of the past with fantastic discernment to get throughout the troubles that lie ahead. As hundreds as you dislike emotional scenes, you appear impelled to get involved with squabbles and arguments among co-employees. It is essential for your fitness which you avoid ingesting at the equal time as you're emotionally disenchanted.

Partnership And Marriage

You take marriage very substantially and frequently decided on a companion who is helpless, lazy and no longer capable of cope. Your inherent desire to nourish and shield induces you to truly be given duties that others will find out now not feasible. You are frequently the longsuffering husbands and wives of the Zodiac, although it isn't on your individual to bitch. You are also formidable to your mate to get on within the world and you do curious approximately your energy to encourage and to assist it. The most cancers girl makes an brilliant partner for guys struggling to get to the pinnacle—specially in occupations that depend upon public help than a Cancer husband. Choose your rightful companion from "Most Compatible Signs" above.

Shared Resources, Legacies, Sex

You have advanced and precise mind of intercourse and the community. You are the form of individual who is a leading advocate of enlightened strategies to abortion, homosexuality, the Pill for young adults and similar topics as soon as now not stated in well mannered gatherings. You also can keep forth with a few impartial thoughts about lack of life and survival and participate in institution inquiries into occult and metaphysical studies. You have strong emotions approximately sharing with others and can visualize a few sort of communal life as a way of human technology.

Higher Development And Long-Distance

Travel

Experience of the excessive attention is not uncommon amongst some of more superior

Cancer kinds. You begin with as an entire lot zest if now not more than the following man or woman to fulfil your worldly interests, but ultimately, you find out that (as you have got had been given often suspected), your fulfilment lies in carrier and surrender of egocentric desires. You have little time for orthodox religions and avoid discoursing with those who divulge dogma. You are a true mediator and religious pragmatist. Less advanced Cancer types are apt to lose themselves in dreaming, wishful questioning and regret.

Public Standing, Career, Prestige   You are a person who has to live with rhythm, the ebb and float of a in particular touchy and indrawn nature with an instinctive out-going urge. You are ambitious and greater eager than some plenty less retiring kinds to get beforehand. You are decided from the start to make a name for your self, and the fact that you don't continuously be successful is not any mirrored photo of your efforts or tenacity. Your frequently competitive pressure permits to catch up on your loss of self-guarantee and herbal reserve. You frequently benefit maritime occupations and people that offer the opportunity to tour, specially remote places.

Friends, Group Activities, Hopes, Wishes

Friendship is one of the important remains of your life. Your buddies are a buffer among you and the realities of the outdoor global. As you stroll out of your house, you need to experience there are various fantastic welcoming and snug locations so you can bypass. You also can stride into the tick of combative truth with an admirable show of aggression, however at the identical time as the day is over, you heal your mental wounds with the aid of touch in conjunction with your pals. You experience supporting your comrades and are the primary to lend coins when you have it. You additionally want to spend money on friends. You tie yourself in your companions with deep bonds of affection and regularly shape lifetime friendships. You are especially dependable and being worried. You enjoy the bodily warmth of corporations and the opportunity they provide to boom your sphere of impact with the aid of discussion.

Hidden Motives, Selfless Service, Psychic Feelings

Despite their overt want for friends, Cancer Ascendant human beings may be some of the recluses of this lifestyles. The power of your feelings, acting on richly inventive disposition, offers you with an inner lifestyles that often techniques self-sufficiency. You analyze greater from watching humans and situations than from formal classes. You have durations of soul-looking introspection. Your more precis mind conflict on the aspect of your sentimental nature, and even as you are sorting the contradictions, you can provide the have an effect on of moodiness. You have sturdy psychic powers and mediumistic capability.

Intuition is greater herbal to you than thinking.

THE LEO CHILD JULY 21 TO AUGUST 21

The Leo child has a big quantity of important and intellectual energy at his or her disposal. Parents and teachers need to appearance that that is directed along first-rate strains. This youngster, because of his forceful dedication, is apt to find out that fulfillment comes pretty consequences. He can also additionally additionally get so carried away with applause and admiration that he overlooks the fee of accomplishment itself.

Young Leo has a natural gift for management and will assert this as his or her right in the presence of other kids. The trouble is a bent to become domineering, to throw his weight spherical unnecessarily, show off and normally bore every person indoors earshot together with his boasting. In a few instances, little Leo will become "little Caesar" and well-known a awesome love of strength, which may be innocent in a baby however is an objectionable excellent in an person.

The Leo infant is an energetic and lovely little man or woman. Quite apart from the early "ego flexing," there may be a dignity and nobility to his nature. His unquestionable braveness turns into apparent early. Although as disobedient as any little one, he is going to seldom resort to mean and spiteful moves. He or she could be able to probable exceptional must be suggested as quickly as that it is cheating to tell reminiscences. This little one's sense of loyalty is ingrained and at times may be carried to absurd lengths.

Leos, are deeply affectionate children, and no matter their love of display and applause, are keenly touchy. Their intuition is frequently top notch They have a excellent feel of pleasure and but are brief to forget approximately about and forgive. Once they make up their minds to perform a little factor, they are unswervingly decided

A Leo toddler regularly acts unexpectedly, specifically wherein satisfaction is worried, locating it very tough to expose down an opportunity to revel in himself. When gambling, he's probably to lose all experience of time and arrive domestic at 9 o'clock at night time for his nighttime meal He has a love of the splendid exterior and is probable to acquit himself nicely the least bit forms of sports activities activities. Young Leo, although taking component in his durations of seclusion, will commonly be decided among corporations and clubs in which he can display his organizing functionality and powers of manipulate.

Parents of Leo teenager need to endeavour to have him knowledgeable in any career or line of tough work he suggests an hobby in. He has a terrific studying capacity, no longer through gathering and memorizing statistics but with the aid of inquiring and know-how its significance. He is in no way certainly happy until he comprehends the motive for an movement or schooling. A herbal commander of men and women inside the making, Leo will in no manner be a shallow echo of some extraordinary man or woman's caprices.

Leo teen has a deep-seated ambition to get to the pinnacle in spite of the fact that she or he might not recognize this internal strength. This infant's massive energies and numerous talents will artwork better harnessed in a particular route, whether or not or now not or no longer in the arts, literature, politics, journalism, era or government management.

Young Leo additionally advantages from an extraordinary instance. Conversely, she or he need to now not be allowed to fall into horrible employer The Leo-Ascendant Personality

You love strength and difference. You achieve success maximum wherein you've got had been given authority. You usually occupy a few excessive or responsible feature in managing or government paintings. You have the present of inspiring others to incredible

accomplishments— until you end up strength happy, wherein case you can cause them to their destroy. You are formidable and confident and fearless. Although high-strung and short to anger, you're very forgiving and don't keep grudges for extended. You have amazing energy and are apt to pour it, without restraint, into an pastime that arouses your sympathy or interest. Therefore you are usually in risk of overdoing things (it is not unknown for a Leo-born to paintings himself to demise).

Although you're usually robust, there may be a wonderful restrict to how far you may push yourself in advance than undermining your health. You have extraordinary need and religion within the future. You are outgoing and magnanimous and scatter your goodwill in all recommendations on the equal time as the whole thing goes nicely. In adversity, you are effortlessly and might seem to withdraw from all other pursuits to take care of one problem. You are not in truth, neglecting any responsibility; you aim to build up the sum of your forces to assault the trouble that occupies you.

You are impatient to come back again to grips with troubles and to put off them. You have the fortitude to undergo significant ache and pain if it's going to bring about a peaceful life. Like the Lion, who's the symbol of this Sign, you're a high-quality fighter, however you want to moreover have your quiet hours lazing inside the solar. And yet again like the King of the Beasts, you're of noble disposition. You have dignity and integrity. You are philanthropic, charitable and constant. You frequently get preserve of favours as regardless of the truth that they have been your due and dispense them with a fantastic deal the same flourish. You are imperious and fond of command. You typically tend to dominate the social sphere in that you glide. You are a bodily appealing and crucial person and gravitate to a characteristic of control as although it were the maximum natural aspect inside the global. You are genuine-natured, generous and kind-hearted. You are also impartial outspoken and at times brutally frank. Your purpose to provide freedom via your capacity to manual, occasionally degenerate into a electricity complex ensuing in an conceited dictatorship. You revel in not anything white as an entire lot as an admiring audience.

Possessions And Personal Security

You are a chunk of a paradox in which cash is involved. You have pretty extravagant taste and but your spending behavior are conservative. You can placed your pennies away with punctilious care and blow the contemporary (well nearly the lot) on a night time time out or a few high priced pricey object. You enjoy manipulating cash and balancing your debts. You can teeter on a razor's factor among real dwelling and financial disaster with an adroitness with a view to make much less confident sorts shudder. Usually, even though, you recognize what you are doing and feature calculated the amount of your assets and reserves right all the way down to the remaining coin. If you get into monetary trouble, you fear continuously and this affects your health.

Chapter 6: Communication With The Environment

Since you want humans to agree with your thoughts, it's miles lucky that you are typically superb at the art of persuasion. You make, in fact, a exceptional salesclerk. Articulate and polished in speech, you've got the knack of speakme your enthusiasm via the energy of your presentation. You are thrilled and tactful. Because you typically accept as authentic with in whatever you advise, you exude an air of sincerity. You are even organized to risk an issue to make your thing.

On the order hand, if you don't believe in what you are pronouncing, the solar air of secrecy has a tendency to evaporate, making you pretty smooth to appearance via. You try to create harmony in your right now surroundings, even to the quantity of bringing like-minded or romantically willing humans together.

Home, Family, Tradition

You insist on being the keep near or mistress of your home. This is probably the reason why most Leonine types do no longer revel in a brilliant quantity of home happiness. You are imperious and pretty conscious of the honour of a wholesome own family tree and the blessings of proper breeding. If your ancestors are unknown tendencies, you're properly set about establishing your dynasty, but modest your situations may be. You are a proud descendant of admirable forebears, you opt to neglect approximately own family skeletons and desire they may depart, You run a good (circle of relatives) deliver and anticipate the unquestioning loyalty and assist of your dependants.

Self-Expression, Love Life, Entertainment Your natural preference and aptitude for being discovered makes it viable that allows you to obtain notable heights of achievement. Although your expulsion to be identified degenerates at instances into showmanship or show-off-manship, you're driven thru the same forces to take benefit of your innovative and finer present day competencies. You will in no manner be content material fabric with what you acquire; you could usually have the conviction that far more possibilities lie interior you-and, for that rely internal others. You are especially capable of instilling exalted thoughts in children and of awakening them to their possibilities. For this cause, you're making an inspiring figure or instructor.

Work And Health

Your profound feel of obligation for some factor gadget you're taking makes you a diligent and industrious worker. Your capability to work hard with revolutionary notion, together at the side of your innate control powers generally guarantees that you get to the pinnacle. Although bold, you are impelled thru the choice to do a challenge for its very own sake. The fact that you could then bask inside the daylight of different humans's admiration is a hidden motivation. Your health can be stricken by overwork, the maximum willing regions being the coronary heart and lower back. Self-self guarantee every so often reasons you to overestimate your powers of physical and intellectual staying power.

Partnership And Marriage

You aren't an smooth man or woman to be married to, notwithstanding the reality that you could be devoted and disarmingly generous. You frequently choose out the incorrect shape of associate. You have a strong steak of independence and a love of freedom, and in case you choose out a mate with comparable developments-as you typically the do-the end result is fireworks. Your imperious nature makes it hard in case you need to percentage authority inside the domestic. You want a royal hassle further to a mate. You are often interested in a innovative type, and this temperament is concept greater for rebellion than servitude. You want an smart partner who is keen and earnest enough to pay the noticeably harmless doses of homage you require in alternate for royal munificence. Choose your rightful associate from the "Compatibility Guide" on web page 10 above.

Share Resources, Legacies, Sex

A degree of sacrifice and ache usually accompanies the Leo enjoy and of sharing. To share with mankind is your finest reason, befitting the son of Sun's Sign. You must learn how to resist the natural urge to use up your energies and ardour in pleasant non-public dreams and concupiscence. You are required often after lengthy-suffering to upward thrust to compassionate heights in which you can renew your self in problem to your fellow man in choice to on your superficial self. You can do this by way of the usage of an immoderate electricity of will to a creative pursuit. Legacies are regularly surrounded via pressured and disordered conditions.

There can be an prolonged conflict to win what you consider to be your rightful inheritance whether or not or not it's far assets, title or the vindication of your own family call. The Leo person commonly succeeds in a few aspect he or she undertakes.

Higher Development And Long-Distance Travel

Your deep routed optimism is primarily based totally completely in particular on religion in your self. And this, in flip, is often supported through the conviction which you are filling a destined role and being guided thru inner forces you do not want to provide an reason behind or understand. It is that this faith, both consciously or unconsciously held, that allows you to anticipate a function of authority or rulership in nearly any scenario. The so-known as divine rights of kings is a postulate and difficult as a manner to apprehend. You need to excursion a ways afield, however you aren't a rubberneck traveler type, you need to apprehend that your journey has a greater motive than mere sight-seeing to make it in reality really worth your whilst.

Public Standing, Career And Prestige

You are a lover of the vestments and tokens of place of business. If you become lord mayor or police chief, you want the 24-carat-gold chain round your neck, the huge barge of the ivory-dealt with pistol. As rapid as you can come up with the money for it, you surround your self with recognition symbols. Apart from creative concerns, all the devices you choose are generally capability, for you appreciate almost as lengthy as it doesn't cramp your fashion. Once in a feature of electricity, you are regularly reluctant to step apart and may ferociously face up to any order to step down. As a superior, you will be one of the boys so long as the men maintain in thoughts you're the simplest. By studying to delegate, You can help protect your health.

Friends, Group Activities, Hopes, Wishes You need a mixed organisation of people around you to stimulate your mind and to save you you from becoming too consistent in your attitudes. You commonly attraction to buddies who, regardless of the fact that they may be overindulgent as an audience, are clever and vivacious. Many of your partners are more youthful, clever and admiring and in this commercial enterprise organisation you allow others to polish beside you with an amused, paternal or maternal beneficence. You are generous in your friends and pick out out the nearest of them with care. Sometimes you best friend your self with humanitarian organization efforts, typically at the organizational facet. Philosophy actions and seminars moreover enchantment to you, however handiest till you may formulate your summary thoughts.

Then you may well set up a "school" of your private.

Hidden Motives, Selfless Service, Psychic Feelings

You every now and then experience neglected and unappreciated and this reasons you to retreat sulkily into yourself. Your towering delight received't permit you to show the reasons (such pettiness is as an opportunity unkindly or is it?), so every person in your vicinity feels a chunk bit uncomfortable without pretty information what. Unless you have got identified with a motive in life you are apt to waft off into incredible daydreams. You have giant capability to serving others selflessly, however once in a while break it through using looking for applause and commendation. You will give up cash but no longer frequently the proper to reputation or hobby. You undergo maximum on the same time as the ones plaudits aren't immediately drawing near.

THE VIRGO CHILD AUGUST 22 TO

SEPTEMBER 22

Virgo youngsters are worriers. They take the smallest disappointments very seriously. They need to be preferred, and but have an unlucky way of horrifying others with the useful resource of being unduly vital and faultfinding. A Virgo infant is regularly exasperated and discouraged thru precise humans's bad reactions to his or her properly intentions, and thru his or her personal aggravated choice to please.

Young Virgo desires to learn how to accessory the wonderful element of his or her nature. Although reserved and modest, those children are manifestly incredible and progressive. They also are keenly clever. But the slightest antagonism and adversity generally commonly tend to deflate them. They live on their nerves to a high-quality amount. They are continually studying one-of-a-kind people's reasons and endeavouring to find out a reason for everything. The sheer impossibility of exceptional this choice explains their simple problem.

The Virgo toddler loves order and technique. Once the ones are installed at domestic or in university, she or he will be able to relax emotionally and rarely be in any problem. But in a disorganized device in which human beings are uncertain, Virgo becomes disoriented. That is why it's frequently a traumatic experience for a Virgo infant or a Virgo man or woman for that don't forget to move to a contemporary domestic, school or method. One astrologer has even claimed you can reason brilliant agitation in a Virgo cat via manner of shifting its saucer! Schoolwork itself, however, is seldom hundreds of a trouble for the Virgo teenager. Along with Gemini, he's one of the best kinds within the Zodiac to teach. He has an inquiring and logical mind, this is usually- looking for to make sensible revel in out of the statistics obtained. Naturally, college instructions make revel in to those boys and girls. They often take a unique hobby in era and mathematics. They are also quite creative and experience devising new strategies of doing topics.

Young Virgo makes friends carefully He's now not a sentimental or emotional character and prefers to choose people on their moves and achievements instead of their terms. He is an idealist and at coronary heart a perfectionist who wants to see everything in its proper vicinity and logical order When he discerns that someone is not being sincere with himself or actual to his type (his intellectual acuity is first-rate), he is going to mention so, no longer with the choice to harm, however to help. This trait is truely frequently misinterpreted, and his playmates can also resent his comments and attitude and ostracize him for them.

The Virgo little one dreams a very good education in order that he doesn't feel no longer as suitable as others. He doesn't, normally, revel in close to physical contact he may additionally experience that cuddling and caressing are pointless and embarrassing. His finer feelings need to be handled delicately and with understand-a way to prevent fussiness and queasiness from turning into consistent in his character. Virgo youngsters are apt to be faddish about sure meals and straight away dislike a few kinds. They can also refuse to consume in an area they revel in is dirty, regardless of the reality that they may be not able to give a conscious reason for this mind-set.

These kids are very brief to take a look at cleanliness and hygiene, but the topics want to not be overemphasized.

The Virgo—Ascendant Personality

If Virgo is your ascendant, you're someone who has an unusual amount of commonplace enjoy. You are a totally energetic reality seeker and attempt to put in force your mind in desire to permit them to be spherical on your head. You goal to "tidy up" your environment to set subjects and people right away; consequently you're now and again perceived as fastidious or hypercritical. You possess a tremendous aptitude for dealing with records, regarding them due to the fact the first necessities for putting in place the order you adore plenty. You are extraordinary at paintings that requires precision and particular abilties. You can be counted at once to have finished your homework properly and to very own a eager idea of sequences and techniques in advance than you begin. You have a look at effects and quick and have wonderful powers of staying electricity. You make a in a feature accountant, clerk, secretary and private assistant. Your very realistic manner of looking at subjects furthermore makes you an in a function worker in more intellectual occupations which encompass foreman, housekeeper, employer orderly or beneficial resource and so on. You aren't without problems contented. Although conservative in outlook, you have got were given a speculative turn of thoughts and frequently turn out to be worrying approximately your affairs. You desire wealth and burn up widespread try building up your monetary savings. You are to your fee range and prudent. You don't enjoy growing a scene approximately cash, however you imply in reality to others which you apprehend what goes on. You are cautiously shielding of your pastimes and also you aren't probable to plunge into economic ventures with out thorough contemplated image. You can also expect to look after the hobbies of others, which makes you a trusted and precious employee, father or mother or associate. You are looking for perfection, no longer a lot in yourself however the outer worldwide. You aim to put everything in its region and are quite methodical and close to to this stop. Your hobby in order extends for your friends and you frequently endeavour to accurate them by manner of manner of putting forward their faults. Despite your nicely intentions, this may be resented. If no longer managed, your impulse to criticize can descend into trifling fault finding. Otherwise, you prefer to continue to be within the records. You are a modest and as an opportunity concerned type, in particular lacking in self-self guarantee. You like to dress neatly or properly however no longer conspicuously. You are diplomatic, wise-and tactful while you need to be. A considerate individual, you are a bargain interested in the look at of diet and hygiene. You are frequently an enthusiastic cook dinner dinner, with a unique bias closer to meals and dishes which might be seemed as contributing to right health.

Chapter 7: Possession And Personal Security

You opt to earn your cash through partnership, via working with or for people. You dislike taking walks by myself. You are happiest making your dwelling in a hobby or profession in which you could observe a straight forward direction, the use of your fantastic aptitude for choosing and filling in statistics as you pass. You are high-quality at carrying out commands. You might make an amazing to pinnacle government. You revel in proudly owning incredible items and will choose to pass over a good deal than to gamble on awful workmanship or inferior super. You apprehend you will be trusted to do a brilliant machine yourself, and you see no cause to just accept a few element a whole lot less from others. You are suitable at balancing budgets and take splendid care to maintain a few thing out of the whole lot you earn. The extravagance of others distresses you deeply if it upsets your monetary affairs.

Communication With The Environment

You are frequently decreasing in your observations. You have a capability for punctuating human arrogance, but this ability to discern sham and self-myth in others isn't typically desired. You might probable make an excellent media critic who is probably counted on to begin public controversy and debate. You are not specifically voluble and may refuse to offer an purpose behind or complex on your criticism. You may be a hint too steady for your opinions. You very own a penetrating commercial organisation mind and are able to smart and subtle exams. You can hastily kind out complex conditions and get all the manner proper down to the nitty-gritty.

Home, Family, Tradition

You are inexperienced at staying inside a fee range, paying bills on time and keeping the home spick-and-span. You experience supervising home and own family affairs. You are deeply aware of the importance of the circle of relatives unit in retaining a wholesome, cohesive and well-ordered society. You have a keen enjoy of morality and might in no way purpose to do whatever that could damage or endanger the traditional family idea. You don't mainly experience being faraway from your family for an prolonged duration. And you are not so keen to tour an extended distance, besides in connection with searching for or moving into a grander or more spacious home.

Self-Expression, Love Life, Entertainment Your method to fulfilling sports is as an opportunity restrained, however the fact that you aren't beyond breaking out on activities. You will be inclined to choose the most secure or greater socially appropriate course, and this will be inhibited with regards to romance and one in all a type interesting diversions. This reserve isn't so advised in Virgo guys as in ladies. The Virgo female may additionally seem frigid and in a well mannered manner unresponsive as a lover due to the fact she is in no way quite exceptional (now not disturbing to find out) wherein her emotions will lead her. The guy is more simply privy to his passionate dreams. When face-to-face collectively together with his spontaneous urges, Virgo person commonly, manage to do the conventionally accurate trouble.

Work And Health

You are an able and chronic employee who might do his or her great to cooperate with fellow personnel. You like being a member of a collection. You percentage your thoughts-regularly actual imaginative without seeking out particular approbation. You excel in laboratory paintings. But a few aspect your profession, you want to surround yourself with the very current clinical device or equipment designed for the technique. You are acutely health-conscious and function advanced views on meals and food plan. You are prone to forget about the fact that the pressure of too much artwork should have an effect to your mainly touchy apprehensive gadget.

Partnership And Marriage

You need a mate who actually appreciates your unflagging efforts and endeavours to carry out your percentage of the good buy. You don't appearance a lot for reward and admiration as for a sympathetic information of your issues. Given the right treatment, you're without troubles soothed and organized to head on serving and strolling with very little grievance. If your associate is not the placid and moderate kind, you're apt to simply accept your lot with quite philosophic resignation. A Virgo man or woman is regularly organized to give up his or her desires to make sure an agreeable and feasible union. Perhaps because of this Virgo isn't always one of the Zodiac's maximum marrying sorts and every now and then makes an early and rigid resolve to live unmarried. Choose your rightful partner from "Most Compatible Signs" above.

Shared Resources, Legacies, Sex.

Sharing is the branch of your lifestyles that offers upward push to interest thru business enterprise, so that you are constantly concerned with possessions, assets and obligations belonging to other people. You are one of the super managers and caretakers of the

Zodiac, as superb from a major or owner.

Concerning sex, the Virgo man or woman frequently regards his or her mind and longings as unwanted man or woman elements and seeks to sublimate them in realistic idea once in a while difficult to apprehend or complicated methods. Virgo humans are usually more concerned with intercourse than the chaste Virgo of life-style implies. Behold their managed outward appearance can be a deep, self-conscious, passion.

Higher Development And Long-Distance Travel

You are inclined to be orthodox in your mindset toward faith and metaphysical subjects. You also can preference to educate of their fields. Although your vision of a particular religion can be considerable and complete, you will probably exercise its tenets in identified procedures. Hence the Virgo character is regularly to be determined conducting a bible have a look at beauty, organizing a church bazaar or giving guidance at a Sunday college. You are keen to decide the deserves of any philosophy or doctrinaire manner of life on its realistic outcomes. Generalities worsen you due to the truth you believe you studied they may be a manner of docking problems. Travel generally holds no high-quality appeal besides as a method of growing cloth holdings or earnings.

Public Standing, Career, Prestige

It is said that Virgo people frequently come to be prominent because of the reality they may be so inoffensive that no person opposes them! This is particularly so in politics, that is frequently a sport of nominating the compromise candidate to keep away from a stalemate. But a person has to carry out the myriad non-first-rate however necessary tasks of the arena together with assembly-line work, clerking and device operating, and no person is extra green or higher perfect temperamentally to the ones occupations than Virgos.

As laptop and digital technicians jogging on small and complex circuits, you're without a peer. You frequently acquire renown through a flair for phrases and consequently makeable editors, newshounds, broadcasters, commentators and so forth. You additionally make pinnacle librarians, secretaries, record keepers and assistants in publishing agencies.

Friends, Group Activities, Hopes, Wishes You want to entertain your friends in an informal environment, ideally at domestic and also you experience cooking for them. You are keenly solicitous of their welfare and fitness and spend a sincere quantity of time doing the rounds on the cell phone and a hint a bargain much less in journeying them at their houses. You experience the employer of homey people. You have an avid hobby in the extremely-cutting-edge dispositions in domestic aids and home equipment.

You like to speak about adorning schemes, furnishings and fixtures. You are not a first rate one for becoming a member of organizations, but while you deliver your phrase, you're a dependable social employee, in particular for disadvantaged human beings, children and animals. You usually private one or domestic pets, to which you are deeply attracted. You are also in all likelihood to guide societies whose goal is to keep antique homes, antiquities and network landmarks.

Hidden Motives, Selfless-Service, Psychic Feelings

You humans with Virgo ascending regularly upward thrust to become a power inside the back of the throne.

Although outspoken and open, you're adept at organizing hobby behind the scenes, at erecting and strolling little structures within the crucial energy form. You frequently fail to accumulate the popularity that your accomplishments entitle you to. It is that this capacity of yours to perform thankless organisation for a very extended length that suits you for a number of the ennobling responsibilities of the arena, inclusive of worrying for the unwell, insane and underprivileged in conditions of obscurity and even penury. This feature self-

sacrifice can produce a deeply religious us of a of mind that works for heavenly rewards and no others.

THE LIBRA CHILD SEPTEMBER 23 TO

OCTOBER 22

The Libra little one is a sensitive flower due to the fact he or she is a assembly thing of thoughts and emotion and people don't combine without problem. The toddler is typically very realistic and colourful however unsure of a way to take care of his or her emotions.

Libras crave love however are reserved and shy about attaining out for it. Consequently, they may maintain close and yet be not able to provide in move back. They are constantly weighing up what to do in their relationship which way to move, what is first-class. The quit end result is that they don't seem to have many responsibilities, and till guided and directed by the use of an facts determine or teacher, may develop up unable to make pleasant use of their many ability talents.

Young Libras don't appear to have plenty energy of mind, mainly for the motives given above. They emerge as excited through an concept, plunge into motion with enthusiasm after which become bored and go looking for a few issue new. If they may't find out some factor precise, they'll lapse into apathy. These kids have little or no urge to growth their abilties; ambition is some factor they need to investigate. They opt to depend on others with out exerting themselves. They want to growth the addiction of operating alongside methodical lines, video games and interests may be used for this. If their hobby isn't maintained via the determine acting as a kind of companion, they will speedy get into mischief.

The practical discern of a Libra teen will recognise right from the begin that his or her infant is artistically willing and that a harsh, uncongenial, immoderate or unpleasant environment will inhibit herbal expression. In such an surroundings, the child is probably to grow to be notably involved and a constant trouble for the determine. But once the innate Libran love of beauty and harmony is acknowledged and cultivated, the potentialities of steady improvement and accomplishment are plenty advanced. For those reasons, the figure have to have a take a look at the child s proclivities inside the youth and coax him alongside in the right path.

A Libra infant is much more likely to become a a success dancer, actor, singer, author, painter, indoors decorator, architect or beauty expert than shine in a cutthroat enterprise career.

Moodiness and jealousy are regularly a problem These kids want desperately to be favored, however their thoughts-set frequently indicates indifference to their playmates. They can be happy and homosexual one 2d, and inexplicably depressed and silent the subsequent. The more they may be left on my own, the extra temperamental and introspective they grow to be. If this is allowed to keep, the kid can also additionally increase up with few friends and unreasonable possessiveness can also cause terrific disappointment in his or her future love lifestyles

Libran children are commonly properly-fashioned and attractive. They have a magnetic appeal that makes extremely good children want to be with them, but they seem no longer capable of preserve the initial attraction. This confuses them. The determine's undertaking is to educate the

Libra infant, with love and understanding, to mix his or her emotional and highbrow sports activities and particular them in unselfish processes consisting of in artwork and social endeavours.

The Libra—Ascendant Personality

You love balance and concord. You are stated to be the judges of the Zodiac, because of your normal attempt to repair equilibrium in a international in which injustice is the norm. You understand neatness and order. Peace isn't always most effective a choice to you, but a deep-seated want. You love companionship and are commonly extremely good, very cautious and agreeably. You are tremendously diplomatic and commonly try to please every person at the equal time. This calculated balancing of the Scales (the symbol of Libra) from time to time inclines you to vacillate.

Not pretty understanding what path to take next, you frequently sit at the fence, attempt to see which manner the wind is blowing, and then jump into the closest bandwagon. You are someone who pertains to as opposed to initiates. You revel in there sufficient reasons inside the international with out your starting up any new ones. You are essentially in opposition to aggravation and are aware about any aggressive go along with the float via the usage of the usage of you that allows you to disenchanted someone someplace. This acute cognizance often makes you mentally indecisive. You are higher tailored to organized placidly and agreeably for activities to arise than to strike out assertively for your self. You apprehend beauty in maximum workplace work, particularly nature, art, track and literature. You enjoy cultured and subtle pleasures and amusements. You are a bright and congenial companion in social situations. You are generally endowed with amazing grace and enchantment, which compliments a well-standard body and symmetrical features. Your preferred companions are happy and thrilled sorts who often own a few creative appreciation of skills. You are an admirer of braveness and exceptional motion in others.

You are idealistic, adaptable intuitive and constructive. A keen belief makes you wonderful at drawing comparisons. You are mainly impressionable, and in case your creativeness isn't always curbed it could leap to dizzy heights of getting a pipe dream, wishful wondering, and impractical responsibilities. You are humane, modest and normally amorous.

Although a very loving individual, you are willing to be changeable. You are formidable but dislike all discordant and unclean varieties of art work. You enjoy getting out and about and feature a enjoy for the social swing. You have right flavor in garments and furniture and enjoy carrying pricey jewellery. Your love of brilliant subjects can bring about extravagance.

Possessions And Personal Security

You hold the info of your economic and assets affairs pretty hidden. Although you can appear like quite open and offhand about these topics, you seldom display screen the true state of affairs. You can secretly be worried about dropping your possessions regardless of the reality that this worry has no actual basis. You revel in dealing in the land in case you get the hazard and are very brief to see a capability good deal or to spot flaws within the profits communicate. Most Libra-born humans spend cash freely and frequently stay beyond their technique. Financial stress can create an intensity in them that can erupt in more extravagance! You experience the consolation of first-rate possessions and prefer to percent this experience with the useful useful resource of giving good-looking objects.

Communication With The Environment

Libra human beings frequently keep a diary approximately their excursion and write lengthy positive letters to their own family and pals. You additionally experience taking snap shots of in that you've had been given been and meting out them to all people who is probably involved. You like to area your itinerary and plans well down on paper and have as many stuff as feasible organized so there are not any slipups. In conservation, you favour broader problems, but there's a risk here that you could recognition on affairs that don't problem you and forget about topics closer to domestic. Sometimes you waste a while and strength gathering and submitting away useless facts.

Home, Family, Tradition

You are admirably inexperienced and prepared within the domestic. You enjoy having matters prepared all of the way down to the very last element so there's an area for the whole lot and at the least litter. If subjects are disordered through no fault of your non-public, you may art work difficult and systematically to repair them to their true u . S . A ., doing this again and again once more if essential. Your persistence wherein your house and family are worried can be pretty splendid. And you extend this pleasant by means of the use of being a conscientious and regulation-abiding citizen. It is critical on your experience of safety to have a home of that you are proud, you seldom surely loosen up till this is executed. You are typically interested in ancestral facts, and if constructing or renovating a domestic, will regularly occupy a tasteful characteristic from the beyond.

Self-Expression, Love Life, Entertainment You are eager to particular yourself thru employer efforts. You favour goals which might be socially well known and, if viable, of super and important gain to the network. Most Librans are deeply sympathetic to the desires of kids—now not always to their offspring. They are often to be determined taking an lively element in mother and father and teachers establishments further to the Boy Scouts and Girl Scouts. In romance, they may be typically guided via way of their head in preference to their coronary coronary coronary heart. They select out to stay aloof from the untidy surroundings that falling in love can recommend. They don't have great get hold of as actual with within the strength in their emotional detachment, despite the fact that they favor to faux to the arena that they do. Sometimes regardless of the fact that, Librans lose their cool in uncommon amorous affairs that produce drastic adjustments.

Work And Health

Physical labour doesn't have a good deal appeal for you. You don't discover it tough to apply yourself for any time frame to mundane or repetitive paintings. You attempt but…it doesn't appear to return off. Any manner you revel in you're equipped for higher subjects than being a cog in a series of wheels, no matter the truth that regularly you aren't effective really what these is probably. You pick out to artwork inside the historic past in which you could carry out a piece thriller string-pulling, manipulating those who perform the greater menial obligations. If you have to, you may come what also can litter through in habitual jobs, the use of your appeal and affable disposition to cover from others, your painful feeling of failure. You frequently undergo bodily troubles introduced about via an lively imagination.

Partnership And Marriage

You are generally higher at introducing harmony into unique people's relationships than into your marital affairs. You have a flair for bringing similar-questioning people together, for combining the one of a kind idiosyncrasies of person into an agreeable concord. You are a tactful matchmaker and dependable mediator. But your marital own family people can be tempestuous. By attempting to preserve a balanced environment for your self, you frequently manipulate to fire up aggression on your mate. You are a natural fighter for the rights of others, and if these can be diagnosed along with your rights, you are truly a effective antagonist. You in fact love peace however no longer continuously at the rate of give up. Chose your rightful companion from "Most Compatible Signs" above.

Shared Resources, Legacies, Sex

The Libra person often draws wealth and affluence with none outstanding striving. The more the ones people warfare to accumulate the possessions of this global, the a lot much less achievement they are apt to experience. Acting alongside preconceived lines of endeavour seems to push the object of their preference further away. Libran once in a while marry for sake of coins and almost unavoidably regret it. Or they'll remedy "in no way all over again" after which repeat the enjoy with the identical result. Despite your pleasant easygoing way, you have got were given have been given a awesome business organisation thoughts. You ought to make cash on the inventory marketplace and in corporate ventures. You additionally stand to advantage via legacies. You normally attain mature age proudly owning pretty big belongings.

Chapter 8: Astrology – Where Starts Everything From…

What is astrology, technological records, esoteric or a human fancy? This query despite the fact that will boom discussions and conflicts among greater conservative, skeptic and academic- oriented people who have touched in a single or exceptional manner the size of non secular and esoteric worlds. It is from time to time possibly this dispute to be quickly finalized.

One of the primary glances of the person modified into his look to the sky and he have become succumbed and curious about its thriller. The primitive man respects and has a veneration of sky-this divine creature. There are lots of property for the astrology foundation, they will be nonetheless debatable so far – whilst, how and why this region has been advanced, and if it is the least bit a technology, faith or philosophy, that could be a disputable query as nicely. Anyhow, most of the ancient and archeological property shows the sturdy relation among the person and the sky.

In the historical instances at the identical time as guy relied exceptional on his self with none sort of technics be capable of facilitate his manner of lifestyles, the simplest and specific reference elements for guy were the marks and emblems of the nature. To orients in vicinity and time the primary movement which he undertakes, seems intuitive and spontaneous, is to have a take a look at the sky. This is his first compass displaying him the route and time. Today we are capable of occasionally endure in mind the worry and understand of the historical guy to the luminous (heavenly) our our bodies and to the nature. His each idea and movement are discovered via rituals and sacrifices trough which he desires to present (reward) his appreciate to the excessive inexplicable forces. He observes and gives account to the movements of the luminous bodies connecting them with tremendous rhythms on the Earth down. After coming across the biking recurrence and reputability of their motions he have become able to degree time. The motion of the most essential luminous body the Sun gives him orientation for the biking reputability of durations of the slight with the intervals of the darkness. He notices that with the motions of the alternative large frame-the Moon, modifications its shape and feature. Something more, luminous body constantly is going again to a decided form after a positive term and starts offevolved the trade of its shape from the start. One of the primary cycles determining the time of looking for the ancient guy have been the degrees of the Moon. This luminary will become a length device of the time. (In the Indo-European languages terms because of this month and Moon are derivatives from the basis "me" which in Latin approach mensis and metior-diploma as properly). On the idea of the night time luminary the number one conceptions seem for the biking recurrence of the existence, for the reincarnation and the karma on the bottom of which simply is assemble the which means of astrology.

In the begin of this era the Sun and the Moon serve the historical man for orientation in time, however step by step the luminous bodies start to serve him as symbols for estimation the most suitable period for agricultural artwork and looking. Even nowadays, in many cultures motions of the Sun and Moon are nevertheless retaining their symbolic and importance for solving (defining) terrific tasks and rituals, mainly for the greater agricultural societies. A present day guy has enough state-of-the-art technics which replaces this archaic method and reveals out gear to overcome, of direction to a pleasing extend the natural failures, however his skip back another time to the man or woman lets in him in a nice way to assess the maximum suitable 2nd of every initiative. Gradually with the time humans word quite some coincidences among motions of the luminary items and activities happening on Earth. People begin to find out and make bigger numerous systems for calculation and interpretation giving them greater protection and peace, in particular in times of over-coming some catastrophe. In this sense, the astrology in its first steps seems lots more religion than a technological knowledge or a kind of social norm. Every luminous body gets a call, rituals and festivities on its event. A lot of archeological sources are discovered these days displaying absolutely independently that during many locations of the place people start to have a look at sky and to make use of the movement of luminous our bodies in a single or extraordinary manner. Following C.G. Jung, each discovery of the human race is staked from the very beginning on the collective thoughts. When man is prepared for superb information, it appears in a manner to be popular, assimilated and realized. The relation among Gods and planets stays contemporary-day up nowadays irrespective of monotheistic conceptions of Christianity (monotheism-religion in a unmarried God) remains stored in lots of cultures- Hinduism, Buddhism and so forth. Together with the awesome festivities and rituals dedicated to the wonderful Gods. And all over again, the distinctive festivities take place in a pleasant time depending on the order of the luminous our bodies. In the most of the ancient civilizations for instants, the cult of the Goddess predominates – the Great Mother, especially inside the agriculture societies wherein harvest is highly crucial for human survival; they control food, fruitfulness, fertility and others. The Moon cycles and its "forever (always) cross again" (having in mind its ranges from new moon at the same time as it is invisible within the route of the opportunity levels until the latest moon all over again) sell (make contributions to) as a stop result the formation of all cosmic-mythological requirements of cyclic move again to the initial factor. All is reversible, each second all begins from the begin. On the premise of the Moon cycles the first standards of reincarnation and karma start to increase –starting, evolution, boom, end result, adulthood, developing older and lack of existence. All what we not prevail to understand right proper right here and now, we'll have the opportunity to recognize inside the next reincarnation (i.E. From the following new moon). The horrific models of conduct, disturbing feelings we're capable of switch as karma to our next reincarnation so one can manage them in a extra positive and wholesome manner.

In later times on the identical time as man begins offevolved to gain greater enjoy and understanding, particularly those which assist him to deal with disasters of the individual and with the caprices of the Mother-Goddess, the sunny and male Gods start to update grade by grade the moon Gods who end up of secondary significance. The incredible Father is raised to eminence, i.E. The thoughts and the logics (the Sun), begin to dominate over the instincts and the unconscious (the Moon). In the mythology of the Solar gods the idea of the cycling repeats as well having in thoughts the movement of the Sun, which passes in 365 days through the twelve vital constellations at a few degree in the whole three hundred and sixty five days. It describes as well the 12 months of the year, the 4 seasons, the solstices and the equinoxes. The Sun and its motion constructing up the photo of the loss of life and constantly resurrecting God.

So for instants, you'll meet a comparable reason nearly in all religions, this is honestly a symbolic reproduction of the iciness solstice (about 22 of December-the shortest day of the 12 months and the longest night) – the begin of a infant who will become Messiah and God, Horus in Egypt, born on 25 of December, Krishna in India, born by way of way of way of Virgin, Dionysus in Greece, born on 25 of December, Mithra in Persia, born on 25 of December as well and so forth. From the summer season solstice (about 22 of June), whilst the longest day of the northern hemisphere is, the day starts offevolved frequently to grow to be shorter (lower) and to emerge as an increasing number of bloodless. People accumulate the harvest and the character prepares for its autumn-winter sleep; the ancients accomplice this phenomenon with the demise. This without a doubt is the lack of lifestyles of the Sun-God. From the date of the wintry weather solstice the day begins offevolved regularly to growth. In the day of the wintry weather solstice the God-Sun is all over again getting born to endow mild, warm temperature and lifestyles. So, the cult to the Sun starts offevolved to put together the floor for modern spiritual requirements and for the repute quo of the patriarchy. People need rituals and rites to honor (appreciate) their God-protector. Thus, all cosmic rhythms and cycles appear to correspond to the human nature and future, humans unconsciously revel in this relation and find out various rituals giving them the opportunity to get in the path of the divine nature. Consciously or now not, man constantly feels his divine nature and appears for possibility to the touch it. When we talk about astrology, each planet is a issuer, of a certain divine element and precept, which we need to combine in our human nature with a purpose to feel us entire and observed out human beings.

Chapter 9: Astrology—Why Believe In It?

There in all likelihood isn't a single astrologist who hasn't heard this query from clients, pals and skeptics. I searched and perplexed for a long time until— and actually all of sudden— the immediate of interest of ways astrology works came to me. Of route, besides in a without a doubt bodily manner, through their magnetic fields, gravitation and rotational orbits, the planets moreover have an impact on us in a completely unconscious, even "mystical" manner. But what shape of a location is astrology really?

At the instant of our beginning, the movement of the celestial our our bodies (the planets) is sealed in a photo of the sky, nearly like a nonetheless image, a photograph, which becomes our inner self, i.E. The outdoor situations will start to healthy our internal attitudes, disposition and being. At the on the spot we drew our first breath, at the same time as the umbilical twine emerge as reduce, we've were given already materialized our soul in a cloth frame. At that point the planets have been placed in a selected way, so as to lay the inspiration for the, so known as, non-public horoscope. When I become born, the Sun turn out to be inside the sign of Aquarius; the Moon become in the signal of Aries, Saturn in the signal of Taurus, and so forth. The horoscope is a synchronous parallelism in time a number of the celestial photo and our start, in an effort to effect our character man or woman. Often humans ask the question approximately our loose will. Do we in reality have one, if the whole lot is predetermined at the time of our shipping? There is once in a while each person, who has unraveled the secret of the Universe, or that of our human destiny. But there may be one thing I can boldly say— certain, there may be a fine predetermination, whether or no longer or not we find it irresistible or no longer. The horoscope suggests to what amount one's functionality may be superior. On the most effective hand, if we try to exceed it, we can undergo, on the opposite, if we don't realise it, we are able to moreover go through. If you plant a seed of an apple, there's no manner it may become an orange. What is essential is how we're going to make use of this functionality and if we can have the need to develop and recognize it.

Astrology is based totally sincerely most of all on the precept of correspondence amongst human beings, the environment and the cosmos—"this, that is up is like this, this is down and this, it's miles down is like this, this is up"—states the precept of Hermes Trismegistus (Hermes the Thrice Great). Hermes's seven ideas, that have reached us thru the a long time, represent the foundation of the esoteric and spiritual know-how (as a minimum that, identified to us). The foundations had been laid about six thousand years within the beyond in historic Egypt. Hermes Trismegistus is the founding father of the Egyptian way of existence and of the doctrine, called "Hermeticism" or "Hermetism." In translation from Latin, "hermeticism" manner hidden, secretive, and mysterious. Hermeticism is hooked up with phenomena like telepathy, magic and everything that research the mysterious techniques and forces, which rise up each in nature and in the guy or women. Hermeticism as a motion includes sciences, like astrology, cabbala, alchemy, and severa unique forms of occult studies and practices.

The seven standards are:

1.The first precept: "The All is thoughts, the Universe is highbrow."

2.The principle of correspondence: "As above, so under; as under, so above."

three.The precept of vibration: "Nothing rests, the whole thing moves; the whole thing vibrates."

four.The principle of polarity: "Everything is dual; everything has poles; the entirety has its pair of opposites; like and unlike are all the equal; opposites are identical in nature, but truly one in every of a type in degree; extremes meet; all truths are however half of of of-truths; all paradoxes may be reconciled."

5. The precept of rhythm: "Everything flows, out and in; the whole thing has its tides; all subjects rise and fall; the pendulum swing manifests within the entire component"

6. The precept of causality: "Every reason has its effect; every impact has its purpose; everything takes region steady with law; danger is however a call for law no longer diagnosed."

7. The principle of gender: "Gender is inside the entirety; the whole thing has its masculine and female precept; Gender manifests on all planes."

As a rely of reality, quite a few the ones necessities were, and hold being scientifically determined via the usage of way of the con-brief researchers and scientists. The step forward in physics, and specially inside the pretty new disciplines of quantum physics and quantum mechanics, is probably clearly beginning to well known the authenticity of these ideas. Another discipline that reached similar conclusions is depth psychology. It appears that psychology (the intellectual international) and physics (the fabric worldwide) collided and the current man commenced out to apprehend the inseparable link some of the spirit, the soul and the body, such because it has been defined loads of years within the past through many religious and esoteric schools. In his studies at the human soul, which he bases on his research of severa religions, cultures and esoteric colleges of idea, C. G. Jung himself comes up with what he calls "synchronicity," which immediately follows from the second one principle of correspondence. "Synchronicity, he writes, is a phenomenon, in which an incidence inside the outside global is meaningfully, however not causally, associated with a psychological nation of mind inside the area-time continuum." (Jung, 2001) He develops the idea that the cosmic cycles do now not form our destiny, but synchronize with it. Jung defines synchronicity because the mysterious connection among the human psyche and the cloth global, considering, of their center, the two are honestly precise kinds of power. In reality, synchronicity is a phenomenon primarily based definitely totally on the principle of correspondence—that, it is above is also underneath, that, that is inner is likewise outside. What precisely does that suggest? Everything that we experience on an inner, intellectual degree is projected out into the arena via symbols. These outside symbols precise the inner technique, which we are going through. For example, perhaps it has passed off to you to reflect onconsideration on a person you haven't seen for a while after which to meet him all of a surprising. Or maybe you study something on a selected problem and then preserve encountering it: you in reality "by using risk" pay attention a few-issue on TV or, once more reputedly thru accident, run during an editorial about it. When you're going through some thing for your existence, you all at once begin strolling into the same difficulty anywhere and, seemingly, the ones "coincidences" are almost typically "accidental." These are, so referred to as, synchronicities. Jung believes that the precognitive dreams are also synchronicities, which reflect the unconscious approaches taking region in every one humans. It isn't an coincidence that there are dreams, which shake us to our center and we enjoy that they mark a wonderful period or event in our lives.

The Western guy is used to paintings with causal relationships. For example, at the equal time as some component takes place to us we commonly ask ourselves "Why is that this taking location to me?" while Eastern philosophy and faith asks any other query: "What goes on handy at the equal time as that is happening to me?" They look for outside symbols on the manner to uncover the mysterious inner manner. By studying the ones symbols, we are capable of get to ourselves and to the voice of our unconscious an entire lot more with out difficulty. They say that symbols are God's language. Dreams are symbolic, the symptoms of ailments are symbolic—for instance, gynecological illnesses in women are often associated with troubles with femininity and so on. Kidney troubles advocate tension inside the sphere of relationships. Even greater telling are the highbrow, or as an opportunity, the neurotic symptoms and signs, like phobias, paranoid neurosis, anorexia, and so forth. You are going through a few element internally and it tasks itself outwardly. For instance, accept as true with that you're going through a intense marital disaster. All of a unexpected you begin to note that maximum of your married friends start getting divorced or talking approximately it. I remember the story of a chum of mine, who got involved with a female, with whom he had a massive age distinction. When the lady had been given pregnant, she determined that she might not keep the little one due to their age distinction. A few days later, my pal shared with me a few component very interesting. He needed to replica a few documents at artwork. When he went to the replica machine, a colleague of his became copying pictures of toddlers. Afterwards, within the night time, he "through coincidence" stumbled upon a film with a story similar to his. Wherever he grew to turn out to be, actually all people became speaking approximately newborns, and then, he knowledgeable me, he knew that his lady friend might likely surrender the abortion. And she did.

When we learn how to interpret the symbols from the outside global that arise in parallel with our internal activities, we can resolve what goes directly to us and why. It is vital to understand that not each prevalence is a manufactured from a causal courting. There are sports activities, which display up proper here and now, and are crucial for our personal boom. Don't look for the motives inside the beyond. However, of route, there also are times, which might be related to the past, i.E. They may be ones of reason and effect. Astrology operates exactly on this principle of synchronicity. Something inner, it virtually is taking location to us on a psychological degree, in our soul, is projected outwards, as outside activities or in the sky, as planetary transits.

Several centuries earlier than Jung, Paracelsus—a Swiss doctor and truth seeker, who lived within the beginning of the XVI century—had a perception, just like synchronicity and the precept of correspondence. According to him, the stellar sky is a cosmic projection of our "darkish psyche," of our subconscious, wherein the archetypes (the photos and the reasons that pressure us) are contemplated through the planets and constellations. Consequently, our horoscope turns into precisely this projection of the region of the planets within the cosmos at the time of our shipping. In different phrases, the whole lot that happens in our lives from this 2nd ahead will correspond to that, which is going on inside the sky and vice versa, and the primary cause for this fact is the right now of our delivery. If we use the language of psychology, we are able to describe it in the following way: the horoscope fixes our psychic reasons and stereotypes of conduct, further to our inherent capability, into area, according with the planets, placed in it, and additives between them.

The planets, in flip, are the symbolic expression of those intellectual motives and desires, which prompt us to extend in a selected route. The actual movement of the planets through the top notch signs of the zodiac will wake up particular instincts and stereotypes, according with which we will react. Something inner, that is going on to us on a mental degree, in our soul, is projected outwards, as activities or within the sky, as transits. The horoscope suggests our, once in a while aware and from time to time unconscious, reasons and goals. This is why I provide an reason at the back of to my customers that the astrologist does not bet or divine. The astrologist merely expresses out loud the subconscious dreams and wishes of the consumer. I inform them, "The astrologist is the voice of your non-public intuition, that you don't want to pay attention."

The 1/3 airtight principle is the precept of vibration: "Nothing is at relaxation, everything is in motion, the whole thing vibrates," it actually is a few different important and fundamental problem of the essence of the field of astrology. Nothing in nature is static; the entirety is in motion (there may be a new, so referred to as, string concept in quantum physics, in step with which everything in nature, from the smallest particle to the most important planet or pressure, is made of strings, which vibrate and consequently create the entirety else). The movement, but, isn't virtually aimless motion; it is associated with improvement, improvement and qualitative adjustments. In technological understanding, there can be the paradigm of evolution, and everyday movement is the vital using strain in the lower back of this approach. The word evolution comes from the Latin evolutio and technique "unrolling" and "revealing." Everything in nature is in movement and, most significantly, develops and evolves. From the very beginning of The Big Bang, in the place of a few minutes, the more youthful Universe come to be born out of a unmarried atom, and later superior to its modern-day kingdom. In a comparable way, the human zygote (the egg, which has been fertilized thru the sperm) develops into an embryo and evolves right into a human. In the horoscope, every trouble has its irradiance and ideas, which emerge as driving forces in a person's development. The horoscope, or begin map, indicates not what a person is like, however what tendencies he should boom, or the frequency, at which he need to vibrate, if you need to really be himself and to develop constructively.

The fourth hermetic precept is set polarity: "Everything is a duality, the whole thing has poles." The opposites are same in of their nature, but first-rate of their level of vibration." Once again, technology uncovers increasingly more convincing records regarding the duality of nature. Nothing within the universe might exist without the principle of duality. Even Plato's and Aristotle's colleges of philosophy are on the two opposing poles, exemplifying the warfare between the cloth and the religious. In the religions of most civilizations, there have constantly existed "correct," or diurnal, gods and "horrible," or nocturnal, gods. The diurnal ones ruled over all matters seen and progressive, on the identical time because the nighttime or underworld (chthonic) 1 ones have been in fee of all the dangerous forces. The historic civilizations, but, identified every types and respected them in addition, without categorizing them through their electricity. They provided sacrifice to each. In the extra cutting-edge-day religions, like Christianity, this assessment is even sharper— Heaven and Hell, the son of God and the satan. So, the dualism has existed ever because the primary, more archaic religions. It is the basis for every effort, each warfare, and every step of improvement. It creates tension between the opposites—day–night time time, yin-yang 2, white-black, love-hate, and plenty of others. This dichotomy can endorse assessment and incompatibility, at the most effective hand, even as it additionally represents complementarity and fecundity, on the opposite. Thus, each planet or sign of the zodiac inside the horoscope can be performed constructively, or destructively. If we have a inclined relationship with the precept and the outstanding that corresponds to a selected planet or sign, we may be complete of hysteria and conflict, however precisely this warfare will generate the vital pressure, which we're capable of need, if you need to begin to paintings on ourselves constructively. If there may be no evil, we wouldn't be able to appreciate the excellent; if we don't stumble upon ugliness, we could not appreciate splendor.

Here we should possibly furthermore issue out the gender precept—"the whole lot has its masculine and woman nature"—that could be a few one of a kind crucial law in nature and, respectively, in the idea of astrology. Everything, like every man or woman, incorporates each the lady and the masculine internal itself. They can not exist with out each unique. Here it isn't the literal man/female idea this is in popularity, despite the fact that they may be a part of the precept. What is meant right here is the masculine in terms of this strength, which creates, which expels the seed of introduction outward. It is always with a plus sign, at the identical time as the girl is the power that is open and welcomes the seed inner its womb, to nurture and to provide starting to, and is generally with a minus sign. In the horoscope, 1/2 of the zodiac signs and symptoms and symptoms explicit the lady aspect, even as the rest are masculine. There is not any horoscope with best feminine or only masculine symptoms and symptoms. If there can be no creation, there might be no lifestyles; if the womb didn't exist, existence might capture to exist.

After our beginning, the horoscope remains like a picture, steady inside the 12 months, month, day and time of our transport. Its strong factor is extremely good. In spite of that, however, the planets do now not stop their movement alongside their orbits however keep on their paths and, in time, undergo each detail of our horoscope, making that, which has been embedded in it as potential, a reality. Life is going on and there can be no preventing it. Every time we obtain equilibrium in our lives, new forces, which disrupt it, seem and provoke us to maintain beforehand. Precisely the fifth precept—"everything flows inwards and outwards, the entirety has its tides; the swing of the pendulum is observed in the entire issue"—describes this periodicity of nature, of the man or woman or ladies and of the cosmos. Everything is rhythmical and cyclical—the changing seasons, the ebbs and flows every month, ladies's menstrual cycle, the alternation of days and nights, and plenty of others. Following their orbits, the planets moreover have their private rhythm (together with the time, essential for a whole revolution across the Sun), and ultimately return to their location to begin, this is their start function within the horoscope, after which begin from the start. For instance, the Moon cycle is ready 28 days; that of Venus is ready 224 days, and so on. Even the maximum crucial organ in our our our bodies, the coronary heart, has its very own rhythm, it's far connected to the general rhythm of the Cosmos, of the cosmic heart. The rhythm is also the premise of song, one of the first human arts. In the start it consisted only of rhythmic tapping with palms and toes, till the number one percussion gadgets had been created. They are the most herbal and primal of human devices; they echo the internal rhythm of our coronary heart and consequently are the primary in our music information.

Time is a few exceptional critical detail in astrology. The second we depart the womb, with our first breath (that is the time (the hour), on which the horoscope is based totally), we start to breathe independently and to interact with the arena spherical us, in incredible phrases, we come to be self sufficient beings, bodily become independent from our mom. This is the at once, in which the situation within the macrocosm will mirror the same one in the microcosm, i.E. Of our soul. Every step of ours from this 2d ahead will correspond to the cosmic rhythms.

Chapter 10: Horoscope – My Authentic Self

At the instantaneous of our beginning we run all through in a selected own family, cultural, ethnical and religious surroundings. So this environment starts to form the first step of our Self thru one-of-a-kind fashions of conduct. Like it or now not, we're precipitated by this environment and regularly we're able to get worried in, to be famous, we begin to reply to its requirements to now not be brushed off or punished. Unfortunately, lots of those outer models do no longer correspond to our actual nature and to our specific goals. The fear of being rejected, mainly through way of our closest human beings -within the starting that is our mom, is deeply implicit worry in all and sundry. Very regularly that is the purpose to overplay, to carry out remarkable roles rather than being our self. Horoscope is the compass that may screen our actual identity, what we're created to be. The greater now preventing this nature, the greater far from our self-self belief, happiness and enjoy of satisfaction. The worst is that we come to be relying at the mood and relation with the surrounding.

Horoscope indicates our implicit functionality, the seed this is sown, but whether or not it'll probable be apple or orange relies upon completely and most effective through our power, the choice and the braveness to broaden up in what we supposed. The horoscope is sort of a manual in the journey of the hero and within the technique of searching of our self in every parents .It indicates our:

Destiny;

Karma;

Personal delusion and project;

Dharma in Hinduism -the placement of our destiny;

Dao within the Chinese concept – the course that we need to bypass.

In highbrow context the horoscope suggests:

The private capabilities of our individual;

The complexes and blockages- as private and general;

Talents and objects;

Our private shadow (our darkish detail) from which we try to break out;

The circle of relatives participants with environment and the opportunity sex;

The existence instructions;

The karma education that we want to find out and live in complete fee

Horoscope is the manifestation of this fate. It includes the general capacity which a person has to release finally of his lifestyles. The hassle is regularly inside the reality that at intuitive degree we feel our future, purpose and capability, but the outside surroundings and instances suppress this internal voice. Most of the horoscope elements are unconscious and wait their time to expose and growth themselves. The quicker we apprehend that, the more we have got the hazard to experience that inner pride and happiness from that we are what we're. I have been searching at this way commonly in my exercise. Often people realize simplest a element of what is at stake in their very very own nature and not even suspect the massive resource of skills and skills which is probably hiding someplace in the darkish in the subconscious. I actually have determined that we have a propensity to get hold to as a minimum one complex element in the horoscope, move deep in there with out a brake and without situation that we're a amazing deal greater wealthy, practical and proficient. Because of one difficult component we pass over treasured opportunities. But from some other component, problems and conflicts provoke us to appearance greater substantially and deeply inner us seeking out answer and answer of the issues. Very regularly conditions display up in which we have issues to take desire. We enjoy frustrated and helpless. But, the whole thing which takes vicinity has a feel and urban that means for our religious and private development and evolution regardless of the fact that of our age. It is specially hard on the equal time as one and same trouble is spherical us and repeats again and again and we are dealing with comparable situations. This can touch one in all a type spheres of life – problems within the human contributors of the family, within the expert and private lifestyles. There are those who normally revel in lonely and cannot meet the proper companion, others who have fears and embarrassments in specific spheres of the lifestyles. Many of those issues have their roots in our adolescence, however now not all of them. There are crisis situations or internal conflicts bothering us; they pressure us to make extreme changes of our mind-set and behavior but commonly we face up to to this alteration. The really one of a type neurosis and stressful states regularly are a source of upper stated issues and initiate them but we do no longer understand it. In this situation the astrology and the horoscope are extraordinarily essential. They show in which the roots of the trouble are, what the which means of the problem is and the manner man can clear up it in his use.

A lot of psychotherapeutics are more and more interest within the astrology at the manner to build up a more whole image approximately their purchaser and a solution of the trouble as well. The astrology appears a completely beneficial tool which serves as a compass of the astrologist and psychotherapeutic to be successfully oriented inside the hassle of the individual that entails him for a assist. There are severa traits and faculties inside the astrology which find out thru the horoscope the psychical country of the person.

For instants, there can be a technique inside the psychology known as Psychodrama which has uses as a history for a current approach inside the astro-psychology – Astrodrama. The founder of the astrodrama is Jeff Jawer. But the most contribution to the astro-psychology has the mind of the Suisse psychologist and psychiatrist C.G.Jung, the founder of the analytical psychology. Jung used the astrological techniques in his investigations and he implements them later in his intellectual hobby. The Jung mind within the astrology amplify similarly the Dane Rudhyar ones and they may be protected in the Bruno Huber School.

Chapter 11: Constructive Elements Of The Horoscope

The astrology works with symbolic language. Every photo has a particular meaning and describes the important energy and precept; if they may be used in a right and whole way, they will open the native ability. Being symbolic, our desires deliver us messages, that would assist us in fixing a tremendous problem if we understand them correctly. Their interpretation is individual and troubles only the dreamer one. The horoscope of a given guy, in a comparable manner is a message which he has to have a look at correctly which will find out the feel and the course of his non-public existence.

According to the hermetic low of the similarity, the standards which form the shape of the solar gadget and manage the motion of the planets impact within the identical manner the formation of the human soul here on the Earth. These cosmic rhythms are inside the basis each of the mythological as of the astrological archetypes, which deeply discovered in our lifestyles in the revel in of deeply nearby motifs and desires. The fundaments of the horoscope are the planets, the zodiacal symptoms, the houses and the additives – or the variety among planets. All the elements boom our DNA of the human nature and psychic. They are the optimistic factors of the horoscope which constructing up our man or woman, our functionality and the path we ought to undergo.

The planets display what inspire us – the position.

The signs and symptoms show how we react – the healthy.

The homes display in which the motion goes on- the degree and the decors.

The elements display how we replicate to the task to expand ourselves.

The planets present one of the maximum crucial factors decoding the horoscope. In astrology one paintings with ten planets - Sun, Moon, Mercury, Venus, Mars, Jupiter, Saturn,

Uranus, Neptune and Pluto. Since the astrology investigates the have an effect on of the cosmos on the Earth, the astrologers use the geocentric tool, i.E. We take a look at the possibility celestial our bodies from the Earth role, from the Sun and the Moon as properly, that is why those luminaries are handled as planets as well. Their role inside the amazing homes and zodiac signs and symptoms and their angular relationships among (additives) as nicely, show the commonplace archetype configuration which constructing up us as particular individuals with all super and "terrible" potentials. The planets in astrology show specific factors of our psychics. They are the movement forces or most important actors at the huge life scene. Every planet describes a particular archetype image or necessity which motivates us to behave in a excessive pleasant way and take the selections. They describe the future and avenue which someone has to pass via.

The elements amongst them display archetype dynamics of the horoscope —who we are and what we assume from the others.

Each of the twelve astrological symptoms and symptoms may be related to the twelve Archetypes or models of behavior. If the planets embodies the archetypal photograph (shape) – father, mother, sister and so forth. Then the zodiac symptoms and signs and signs will display us how (behavioral) this image will appear. The moon is usually associated with the image (imago) of the mother or with what we search for and discover in it, but it is going to be one-of-a-type in every zodiacal signal.

For instants, the Moon in sign Gemini speaks to us approximately the emotionally far flung, however very shrewd mother who inside the most times behaves extra as a chum and inside the uncommon times as a mother. The Moon in Cancer will recreate without a doubt one-of-a-type wonderful form of relation – picture of mom – caring, slight and so forth.

The houses of astrology describe the area where the planets located their energy. The elf houses represent diverse outside fields if the human lifestyles. They are related more with the outdoor surroundings and conditions than with our internal scenario

SHORT DESCRIPTION OF THE HOUSES

The Ascendant is one of the most critical factors in the horoscope. It symbolizes our thoughts-set each to ourselves and to the sector. The Ascendant shows how we express our individuality. It serves as a masks that protects us from the annoying conditions of the out of doors global. This is our personality or face that we show to others, in advance than show our right self.

1st House - Nature - describes the appearance, conduct, temperament, physical health of a person. The first few years after start.

second House - Possessions - describes our non-public property and ability, in addition to facts (material, physical and highbrow); possessions, safety and loss.

0.33 House - Communication/Relatives - describes our manner of speakme and gaining knowledge of, preliminary training, the nearby environment, brothers, sisters; nearby journeys.

4th House (IC)- Home/Roots - describes the residence surroundings in adolescence, the figure of the opportunity sex, and our dating with him, circle of relatives traditions, the past, the residence wherein we live as tons as the give up of life.

5th House - Creativity/kids - describes how we express the real "Self". Creativity, coronary coronary heart and loving, relationships, youngsters and our attitudes to them; recreation and entertainments.

6th House - Service/Health - describes the ordinary life, work, health, and the way a person takes care of himself and others; hygiene, nutrients and diets.

7th House (Descendant) - Marriage/partnership - describes the marital and commercial enterprise partnerships, circle of relatives and intimate relationships, open enemies, the target audience.

eighth House - Death/Reincarnation/Foreign assets - describes the crucial and close to-demise reminiscences, death, reincarnation and transformation, intercourse and concept. Occult pursuits; Investments, insurance, inheritances; surgical interventions.

ninth House - Long journeys/Expansion - describes the distant places international locations and manner of existence, higher education, philosophy, religion, journey.

tenth House (MC) – Career - describes expert dreams, social popularity, social life, achievements, the determine of the alternative intercourse.

11th House - Friends /Hopes - describes the collective art work, friends, prolonged-term desires and plans, the lovers, the corporations and ideals.

12th House – Karma/ the non secular path- describes the transcendent, religious life, the unconscious, the fears, loneliness, hospitals, prisons, secrets and techniques and techniques and strategies, break out.

Aspects (angular relationships) some of the planets, especially those to non-public planets show how engage the severa planetary standards. The primary factors with which it definitely works in astrology are so called maximum vital elements – conjunction (0º), opposition (180º), rectangular (90º), trine (120º) and sextile (60º). Other minor components add most effective the shades to the overall photograph.

Chapter 12: Astrology And Psychology – The Balance Between Spirit, Soul And Body

Psychological astrology is human oriented, i.E. Directed to the troubles of character and their solving. This is a fairly new vicinity – the department in astrology, regarded within the 60 years of the ultimate century. Perhaps one of the founding fathers of mental astrology is Carl Gustav Jung who in the later levels of his psychiatric exercise is inquisitive about the esoteric, particularly medieval Alchemy and subsequently to astrology. Working collectively with schizophrenics, he discovers sincerely how wealthy is the internal worldwide of these people. Many of them who have been really unenlightened in episodes of psychotic seizures mythological recollections cautioned him, with out ever have the idea that they clearly exist. This brings him deep an archetype symbolism of repetitive and well-known photos embodied in all people, no matter, race, way of life or non secular affiliation.

Directing his interest in astrology, he discovers that horoscope is a symbolic photo of our own psyche with all our wishes and hopes. In mental astrology is tested more unconscious techniques that run inside the guy himself. These techniques are "responsible" for the external occasions that take area to us, but earlier than we play them inside the out of doors global we enjoy them internally. For example, if someone modified into born on a entire moon, astrological, due to this in his transport the Sun and Moon will be in element opposition. In classical astrology this element is interpreted due to the fact the divorce of the mother and father, and later may have an impact on the divorce of the man or woman himself in his vintage age. So interpreted, however, has no useful facts. He truely waits for the event speedy or past due to stand up. In mental astrology, astrologer's purpose is to direct the attention of guy inwards in the direction of himself and tells him that he has an internal battle that would treatment. If the Sun is the image of our consciousness and Self, then the Moon symbolizes the unconscious, instincts and the strategies that run below the brink of popularity. When we interpret that the two Luminaries are in opposition, i.E. One hundred eighty ranges from one another, obviously a person slamming most of the 2 traits – his mind and Self need one, but unconscious "thinks" in any other way. And because of the truth the Sun and Moon is the traditional wedding ceremony couple (hieros gamos) 3 – Husband and Wife, inside the real international this opposition can also additionally play out as a real divorce between man and his accomplice. But if you work at the inner quandary, there are actual possibilities to remedy this war. Here's the way it works, the psychological astrology. Thanks to her, you may music the unique highbrow complexes, lousy patterns, even more extreme neuroses, which worsen the fine of human lifestyles. While the motive of the symptom or problem inside the horoscope can be determined very with out troubles, the psychotherapeutic will want psychologically pretty some time until he reaches the center of the struggle. The more we are clueless, suggest that outside sports have an impact on us and "manage" our lives. When we have been younger, we run at some point of in a given surroundings that places us any necessities to our version of behavior. So we sense forced to answer the ones expectations now not to be rejected through our favourite humans and from our midst. Unfortunately part of our actual nature, we positioned reluctantly and start to play the sport. But a few thing we suppressed does no longer exist in a peace, in the long run it will draw our hobby after which began out out our actual boom and reputation of ourselves and of the world. The horoscope might also furthermore exactly display the ones latent skills of our person, abilities and potentials that want to installation that allows you to be in sync with the actual nature. Otherwise, permit the inertia and the chaos of life. Psychological astrology helps us to look the ones elements of ourselves, and if we understand them as ours and integrate them, then we have already got the control over our life. Everything that we don't apprehend in ourselves comes into our lives within the form of humans and sports. For instance, if, deep down, we had been suppressed anger and now not admit it overtly, then our lives will continuously draw it within the form of aggressive people or activities in an effort to supply us to a rage. If we suppressed our aggressive and cocky individual, we are able to continuously confront collectively with her and with such individuals who will provoke us to boom this a part of our nature. When we apprehend that the ones features are ours, then there may be not want outside events to "pressure" us and we are able to be able freely to have this wonderful.

Psychological astrology works with all factors within the horoscope and all relationships as in Classical Astrology. Unlike the latter, however, this new location breaks the entirety through the prism of human psychology, and those are our desires, longings, potentials. Its reason is to direct the eye of the character to the conclusion of those skills, no longer to anticipate the whole lot on a platter. To reply to our horoscope that permits you to set up it, however, calls for lots of power, staying strength and self perception. Much less hard is the astrologer to tell us what will seem and genuinely wait, but then give up all our electricity and manipulate in his arms and in the hands of chance. But if we need to revel in the reference to the real roots, with the middle of our authentic Self we need to enlarge and to position our efforts into an prolonged-term purpose.

In the concept of intellectual astrology is enshrined the life cause that the whole thing relies upon on us and on our hard work. Any capacity hiding within the horoscopes will take the time to discover it and recognize it. Each issue inside the interpretation of intellectual horoscope is considerable and consists of information about in which and the way to artwork to be ourselves. Often it is so contrasting challenge subjects and tendencies, which is probably difficult to describe, but what approximately if we need to reconcile and integrate them into our personal nature. The greater the stress, the greater is our capability.

Chapter 13: Birth Of The Hero

THE ELEMENTS

THE START OF THE JOURNEY

Everything in our existence has a beginning, has an give up. Go somewhere to get the aspect that we were speeding. However, in advance than us to be what we're, we need material-primary energy which builds tissue, the DNA to grow to be your self. Scientists have decided how our universe started out, proved (as a minimum for now) that every one started out out out from the element, much a lot much less than an atom, which end up natural power and capacity that consists of all information approximately the entirety that exists inside the Universe. This Big Bang made the beginning of what we've were given emerge as. Everything we see, touch or enjoy with our senses is descended from there — large and dramatic explosion. Esoteric talk about two levels of situation — one is the fabric, the opposite non secular, every exists integer inside the worldwide which furthermore applies to us human beings.

On the only hand we've got a fabric frame, on the opposite we've got non secular or as they name it the strength body. Both styles of circumstance are made out of fabric, taken into consideration surely considered one of which we will touch and enjoy, and the opposite we are capable of most effective perceivable via manner of the senses and instinct. But both manifestations include in themselves and are made from power, as everything else within the Universe.

Astrology does now not make exceptions in this recognize. Its basis is based mostly on the energies and their combination in particular manifestations, which ultimately encompass in us as humans, manufactured from flesh and blood, in addition to in our intellectual and religious needs, in our spirit and soul. The foundation on which the astrology is constructed up are the factors, from which in the end starts offevolved all. This is the number one material, this is answerable for our life. Astronomers declare that we're manufactured from megastar dust, i.E. Descended from the celebs, manner to their nuclear fusion, the manner that takes region in the Sun and paperwork numerous chemical elements, and this is herbal electricity. So the factors can also be in assessment with this nuclear manner; from their clash with one another to shape the number one materials vital for our life.

On this basis lays all of astrology. These element statistics is of vital significance for the information of this discipline. Esoteric schools say that the universe is constructed from them. Each of them is part of the composition of every dwelling creature or item and approximately the universe from micro to macrocosmic. For instance, the concept of the elements is based totally mostly on 5 factors: water, hearth, wood, metal and earth. These factors have set up hyperlinks with whenever and space. The 5 factors have interaction continuously to one another, one begets the alternative, or every different are destroyed. In western civilizations and particularly for the Greeks, the factors are four in variety – fireside, water, air and earth.

In the identical manner, much like the idea they have interaction to each other as are destroyed, or provide rise to every different. You can not forget the motion of yin and Yang, i.E. Male and female manifestation, which in aggregate with elements symbolizes the complexity and the limitless variety of creatures, thru movement and the transformation of the elements. The exam and have a look at of things in astrology has its origins in the teachings of the awesome philosophers Pythagoras, Plato and Aristotle. According to their doctrine, in preferred the numerous sports and techniques in life boil proper proper all the way down to the manifestations of the factors that outline the essence of herbal forces. Each element originates from primary ideas:

Water – has its origins within the cold and dampness;

The air from humidity and warmth;

The fireside from the warm temperature and dryness;

Earth from dryness and bloodless.

In many cultures, religions or teachings elements are at the middle of the diverse natural, religious and psychological manifestations and phenomena. In the historic Chinese conventional ebook of adjustments or I Ching (prediction tool) is based on woman and male – Yin and Yang and the corresponding factors. The sixty 4 hexagrams are a aggregate of Yin-Yang-sky and Earth energies, in addition to fireside, water, thunder, wind, tree, mountain, lake, swamp. In almost every mythology, no matter way of life and civilization, each divine image turned into related to the corresponding element. The origins of the area have been designed on the sport a number of the elements. In the severa myths about the introduction delusion tells how mother earth emerged from the chaos – which is nearly constantly associated with the Ocean (water) – and mated with the God of the sky (air) and from their union had been born the flowers, beasts and birds. For instance, Indian ethnicity, the Navajo creation fable tells how the writer via his mind created the mild of East (this might be associated with the growing of the Sun), then this belief headed south and created the water, then headed west and created the air, on the equal time as the North produced pollen. These four factors are the concept for the beginning and development of the location. In the various thriller societies, the method of initiation have come to be additionally associated with passage through the 4 factors, as a sort of purification and enlightenment. For instance, within the preliminary rituals of masons, the newly hired comes first from the floor then receives purified the air passing thru the water and hearth (Chevalier Jean, Gheerbrant Alain, 1995).

Other elements constitute one of the fundamental situations: liquid, gaseous, fiery and firmly, as every u . S . A . Has a wonderful level of manifestation. In principle, the begin of the cycle starting from the number one detail – water and ends with the ultimate – Earth passes via intermediate air and fireplace. Water as a picture of para fabric is the winner of the DNA code needed for any lifestyles.

The give up of the cycle is related to the Earth element, it's the photo of materialization proper proper right here on Earth, thru which we exist in our our bodies

Air and hearth are the elements which may be associated with transformation and conversion of one country to some other (fireside) and the appearance of hyperlinks the various diverse factors to be combined in a unmarried entire (air). This version of the 4 elements and their cycle is not random. In this manner produces a famous model of nature, and of human temperament. This version we're able to format on the ranges of human life, in which all the passing of kids to antique age – spring, summer time, autumn and iciness; from midnight till sunrise, from dawn to midday, from noon to sundown, from sundown till nighttime. Not by using threat, the astrologic wheel is break up into 4 quadrants as properly. Thanks to the diverse combos of the factors start to beginning and zodiacal signs and signs and symptoms and signs and symptoms, which all are widely known. Zodiac signs and symptoms and symptoms are a mixture of ardour and fantastic, further to male or lady respectively, therefore representing the inherited sample of conduct. However, each element has a certain amazing that makes it unique and irreplaceable. The functions with which it surely works in astrology are cardinal, consistent and mobile. So every element with the corresponding quality will supply starting and zodiac signal. In addition, we are capable of add one greater fundamental and crucial for the person and the area, and it is a division of polarities – men's residence and feminine. So every unmarried man or woman has specific polarity male or woman, and applicable trends of those phrases. For example, the zodiacal signal Aries is a mixture of firebending, the cardinal first-rate and man's residence and there may be no any other man or woman with the equal traits that makes all and sundry very precise.

The Group of factors can be defined as a psychological type and temperament, and houses which embody the form of motivation.

The elements are the essential rely, pram-cloth, from which the sun hero draws electricity and capability from the moment of his shipping. He unconsciously will recognize those styles of conduct and desires, at the way to provoke him to a one-of-a-kind mode of behavior, response and boom. He couldn't be so unique and unforgettable with out the combination of the factors, due to the reality planets in astrology are the photograph of certain photos and archetypes, while the mixture of the factors will show the modes of conduct, needs, and reaction in every human beings, and it is particular for every character.

Before we dive into the heroic journey of the solar hero is right to find out fireplace as temperament and psycho-logical kind, so you can help us deepen our understanding and instinct on the subject of ourselves. The factors are the motive that provokes us to dive in a unmarried or a few different journey that lets in you to display the splendor and richness of our non-public unique nature. The zodiac signs and symptoms and signs and symptoms of the elements are the nuances, tones and semitones of existence. Without them we could not have a choice and splendor. Each individual has specific combos of things. For some human beings prevails one or the other one that motivate them to a great way of conduct. Every man or woman is so rich. It is the company of severa and particular competencies that expressed constructively the advent of a totally unique and stylish photograph. Each element brings a quality message which read effectively can more completely to supplement and diversify the person and our lives. Often but suppressing excellent components of our nature, injuring the integrity, which we feel inferior and incomplete. So the extra we open our senses to sense the strength of every detail, the greater we realize the individual of our true nature.

Sometimes the distribution of every detail in our Horoscopes is special one prevails at the charge of a few other, which leads to imbalance and instability in temperament. Sometimes you may even miss any of them, that consciously or not try and compensate through the use of attracting into our existence human beings, bearers of the lacking detail, and regularly even choose out a career close to it. Whatever, but, is their distribution their understanding will permit us to apply the building of the qualities and their capability in useful manner.

www.ingramcontent.com/pod-product-compliance
Lightning Source LLC
Chambersburg PA
CBHW071442080526
44587CB00014B/1959